TRAV

Costa del Sol

p

BAR

TRAVELBUG
Costa del Sol

Edited, designed and produced in 2006 by Automobile Association Developments Limited for Parragon, Queen Street House, 4 Queen Street, Bath BA1 1HE, UK

Published by AA Publishing (a trading name of Automobile Association Developments Limited, whose registered office is Fanum House, Basing View, Basingstoke, Hampshire, RG21 4EA. Registered number 1878835).

ISBN-10: 0-7495-4640-9
ISBN-13: 978-0-7495-4640-3

Material in this book may have appeared in other AA publications.

A CIP catalogue record for this book is available from the British Library.

Printed and bound by Everbest, China

Find out more about AA Publishing and the wide range of services the AA provides by visiting our website at
www.theAA.com

A02441

Contents

KEY TO SYMBOLS

Throughout the guide a few straightforward symbols are used to denote the following categories:

- address or location
- telephone number
- opening times
- restaurant or café on premises or near by
- nearest underground train station
- nearest bus/tram route
- nearest overground train station
- facilities for visitors with disabilities
- admission charge
- other places of interest near by
- tourist information
- other practical information
- ➤ indicates the page where you will find a fuller description

This book is divided into six sections to cover the most important aspects of your visit to Costa del Sol.

Essence of Costa del Sol pages 10–11

10 Top Tips pages 12–13

10 Top Places pages 14–37
Our choice of the Top Ten attractions in Costa del Sol, with practical information.

Discover pages 38–193
Two sections: Málaga and Costa del Sol & Beyond, each with brief introductions and a listing of the main attractions

Practical information
4 suggested walks
4 suggested tours
Listings of the best places to eat and stay

Shopping and leisure pages 194–231
Listings of the best places to shop, take the children and be entertained.

What you need to know pages 236–49
A practical section containing essential travel information.

Maps
A list of the maps that have been used in this travel guide can be found in the index on pages 250–53.

Prices
Where appropriate, an indication of the cost of an establishment is given by **€** signs:
€€€ denotes higher prices, **€€** denotes average prices, while **€** denotes lower charges.

The Costa del Sol is essentially about year-round fun and sun. With its long beaches, restaurants, bars, and choice of entertainment, it caters for all markets, from luxury to package tours. You can go for action, play golf or tennis, pursue your favourite water sports, or opt for the sweet life – poolside sunbathing and leisurely lunches by the sea or on a balcony, delightful on a warm, sunny day.

10 Top Tips

If you only have a short time to visit Costa del Sol, or would like to get a really complete picture of the region, here are the essentials:

- **Do the daytime scene** in Puerto Banús. Linger over a drink at the Sinatra Bar or the Saladuba Pub and admire the yachts. Then move on for a long lunch at one of the stylish open-air restaurants on the quayside.

- **Enjoy fresh seafood** at any one of the *chiringuitos* (beach restaurants) in La Carihuela, Torremolinos.

- **Wander around** the picturesque old town of Marbella and round off with a drink in the Plaza de los Naranjos.

- **Visit Málaga** and do an evening round of the wealth of *tapas* bars centred in the old town.

- **Walk up to the Alcazaba and Gibralfaro** for the panoramic views over Málaga and the bay.

- **See a flamenco show** in Málaga or inland in Sevilla.

- **Have an evening drink** on Marbella's promenade and watch the sunset, taking in a wide view of the Rock of Gibraltar and coastline of Africa.

- **Do the rounds of Banús by night**. The action starts around midnight and continues until dawn with dozens of discos, bars and clubs. Take your pick!

- **Drive up into the hills** to Mijas and enjoy the magnificent views.

- **Visit Ronda** to admire its stunning setting and famous old bridge, subject of countless paintings and photographs. Highlights include visits to the Alhambra in Granada, the Great Mosque at Córdoba and Sevilla, capital of Andalucía.

10 Top Places

La Alcazaba Málaga

The old Moorish fortress or *alcazaba*, dating back to the second half of the 11th century, stands high above the city of Málaga.

Just up from the Plaza de Aduana are the fortified walls of La Alcazaba, landmark of Málaga. The fortress dates back to the 700s, but most of the structure belongs to the mid-11th century. Entrance is through the gateway, the Puerta del Cristo (Christ's Door), where the first Mass was celebrated following the Christian victory over the town.

The way winds up through attractively laid out gardens and fountains, passing through the gateways of Puerta de las Columnas, Arco del Cristo and Arcos de Granada. Terraces offer magnificent views of the town and harbour. A small palace within the inner perimeter is the home of the Museo de la Alcazaba, which displays a range of Moorish artefacts recovered from the area.

Below the entrance to the Alcazaba are the ruins of a Roman amphitheatre dating back to the second century AD.

Parts of the old structure can be seen with restoration continuing. Above the Alcazaba stands the castle which crowns the Gibralfaro Hill (➤ 48).

✉ Calle Alcazabilla, s/n ☎ 952 22 72 30 🕐 Tue–Sun 8:30–7 Inexpensive Centro-Alameda railway station ♿ Lift up to Alcazaba, entrance behind the Town Hall (Ayuntamiento)

ℹ Málaga (➤ 43)

La Alhambra Granada

One of Spain's greatest splendours, the world-famous palace of La Alhambra remains as a legacy of the rich culture brought to the peninsula by the Moors.

The Alhambra holds a commanding position above the city of Granada, backed by the peaks of the Sierra Nevada. In 1984 it joined UNESCO's list of World Heritage Sites. Built by the Moors between the 13th and 15th centuries, it was used as a residence by Muhammad I, and members of the Nasrid dynasty.

Walk up to the entrance from the Plaza Nueva. To the east is the Renaissance palace of Emperor Carlos V, which was started in 1526 but never completed. To the west stands the Alcazaba, the oldest building on the site. Climb up to the top of the Vela tower for breathtaking views of Granada and the Sierra Nevada.

A tour of the interior of the Casa Real (Royal Palace) reveals the true marvels of the Alhambra: the beautifully decorated Patio de Mexuar, the attractive Patio de los Arrayanes

(named after the myrtle trees which line a rectangular pool), and the sumptuous Salón de los Embajadores (Ambassadors' Hall) with its richly carved and coffered ceiling. The Sala de los Abencerrajes has an impressive stalactite ceiling, and the Sala de las Dos Hermanas (Hall of the Two Sisters) features a delicate honeycomb dome. The focal point is the Patio de los Leones (Courtyard of Lions) named after the 12 figures which surround the central fountain.

On the nearby Cerro del Sol (Hill of the Sun) stands the Palacio del Generalife. Dating back to the early 1300s, it was the summer palace of the Moorish kings. The gardens exude an aura of romance, with pools and fountains amidst greenery and flowers.

✉ Calle Real, s/n, Granada ☎ 958 02 7900 ⌚ Mar–Oct daily 8:30–8. Night visits Tue–Sat, 8:30–6. Fri, Sat 8–9:30. Access to the Palacios Nazaries 8–8:45 ✋ Moderate (free for the disabled, senior citizens and Sun after 3pm) 🚌 Alhambrabus from town centre ? Advance booking is strongly recommended. Reservations can be made through any branch of the Banco Bilbao Vizcaya Argentaria (BBV), or ☎ 00 34 915 37 91 78 from outside Spain, or 902 22 44 60 inside the country. A limited number of tickets are sold daily on site but sell out quickly.

Casares

With its mass of whitewashed houses sprawling up the hillside, Casares has acquired a reputation as the most photogenic town in Andalucía

From whichever angle you approach, the views of Casares are spectacular. The town is easily accessible from the coast: a turning from Estepona leads up into the hills of the Sierra Bermeja. While the drive itself takes you through a scenic route of hills and woodland, nothing prepares you for the view of Casares with its white houses spread over the hill and crowned by an old Moorish castle. Casares saw many battles between the warring Moslems, until it was taken by the Christians in the mid-15th century.

Discover the charm of Casares by strolling through its white, terraced streets to the castle above. The fortress was built in the 13th century on Roman foundations.

The views become more spectacular as you continue to the summit, where you will be rewarded by a panorama over olive groves, orchards and forests, to the blue of the Mediterranean Sea.

✉ 105km west of Málaga 🚌 Local buses ❓ August Fair (early Aug)
ℹ Tourist information: Calle Fuente 91, Casares ☎ 952 89 41 26

Cuevas de Nerja

This series of caverns, close to the coastal town of Nerja, contains spectacular rock formations, and palaeolithic paintings (not open to the public).

These limestone caves were discovered in 1959 by a group of boys who were out exploring. Beyond the first grotto, great caverns revealed a wonderful world of stalactites and stalagmites, wall paintings, stone tools and fragments of pottery. Investigations by experts show that the area must have been inhabited by man over 20,000 years ago.

The rock paintings are not open for public viewing, but photographs of them are on display. For the tourist, however, the attraction lies in the magnificent display of formations which are enhanced by special lighting effects.

The first chamber provides a magnificent setting for concerts which are held here as part of an annual summer festival. The next cavern is called the Hall of Ghosts after a strange shroud-like figure which appears in the stone. Most impressive, however, is the huge Hall of Cataclysms, which has a tall column rising from a mass of stalactites.

✉ 4km east of Nerja ☎ 952 52 95 20 (in Nerja) 🕐 Daily 10–2, 4–6:30 Inexpensive Restaurant (€€) Best by car ? Summer concerts and ballet performances ℹ Nerja (➤ 127)

La Giralda y La Catedral Sevilla

The minaret tower known as La Giralda, seen as a symbol of Sevilla, rises proudly above the great cathedral, third largest in Europe.

The 98m-high brick tower of La Giralda is a prominent feature of Sevilla. It was built in the 12th century as the minaret of the former Great Mosque. In 1565 a section with 25 bells was added and topped with a bronze statue representing Faith, which acts as a *giralda* (weather vane). Climb up to the belfry for magnificent views over the city.

The grand cathedral was built in the Gothic style, with some Renaissance influences. The interior is awe-inspiring for its sheer size and the richness of its decoration, with Gothic columns supporting massive arches which reach up to the great heights of the vaulted ceiling.

A handsome 16th-century Plateresque grille in the Sanctuary encloses an immense golden Gothic altarpiece which rates as one of the cathedral's greatest glories and is said to be the largest altar in the world. Started by the Flemish

artist Dancart in 1482, it took almost a hundred years to complete the 45 tableaux depicting the lives of Jesus and Mary.

The choir stalls are fine examples of Flamboyant Gothic. Notable also is the Capilla Real (Royal Chapel). Completed in 1575, it features a richly decorated Renaissance cupola. In the south transept lies the ornate tomb of Christopher Columbus, whose body lay here for a time after it was transported from Cuba.

✉ Plaza Virgen de los Reyes ☎ 954 21 49 71 🕐 Mon–Sat 11–5, Sun 2–6 Moderate; Sun free RENFE station ℹ Sevilla (➤ 142)

La Mezquita Córdoba

The great mosque of Córdoba is a unique monument which stands as a remarkable achievement of Moorish architecture.

The Mezquita of Córdoba was built in four stages between the 8th and 10th centuries and features amongst the world's largest mosques. It remains a testimony to the immense power of Islam at the height of its domination of the peninsula.

Do not be discouraged by the mosque's somewhat forbidding outward appearance: its beauty lies within. The main entrance is through the Puerta del Perdón, which leads into the Patio de los Naranjos (Courtyard of the Oranges). Once inside you will be confronted by myriad columns of onyx, marble and granite. The light effects within

this dim interior are sensational. The columns are topped by decorated capitals and crowned by the striking red-and-white arches so characteristic of Moorish architecture. There is a sense of awe and mysticism, special to this particular mosque, which lures the visitor back time and time again.

To find a Christian cathedral within the very heart of the mosque comes as something of a surprise. It was built in the 1520s on the orders of Hapsburg Emperor Carlos V, who later regretted his decision. However, it does blend into its surroundings.

Rising above the Puerta del Perdón is the bell tower, which offers splendid views.

✉ Torrijos y Cardenal Herrero ☎ 957 47 05 12 ◷ Mon–Sat 10–7, Sun 2–7 ✋ Moderate 🚉 RENFE station, Avenida de America, Córdoba ℹ Córdoba (➤ 95)

Casco Antiguo Marbella

The jewel of Marbella is its Casco Antiguo (Old Town), a picturesque maze of narrow streets, pretty squares and whitewashed houses.

Located to the north of Avenida Ramón y Cajal, which cuts through the town, Marbella's old quarter is a delightful area in which to browse. Among its prettiest streets are Remedios, Dolores, Rincón de la Virgen and San Cristóbal which are noted for the brilliance of their flower displays.

The Plaza de los Naranjos is a charming square lined with neatly pruned orange trees. This is a popular place for a drink or an alfresco meal where you can enjoy its lively atmosphere.

Evidence of Marbella's Moorish, Christian and Roman past can be seen on many of its buildings. Take a look at the Iglesia de la Incarnación and, above it, the remaining towers of an old Moorish fortress.

☒ Marbella (56km west of Málaga) 🚌 Marbella bus stop, Avenida Ricardo Soriano 21 (Bus station Avenida del Trapiche s/n) ☎ 952 76 44 00) ? Pre-Lent Carnival; Fería de San Bernabé (11–18 Jun)

Mijas

Despite the fact that Mijas caters so obviously for the tourist it has managed to retain its charm. The little town is undeniably picturesque, with its white houses, narrow winding streets, flowers and plants. The setting is most attractive, offering magnificent views of the pine-clad mountains which surround it and the coast below. Furthermore, its proximity to the coast, a drive of some 20 minutes or so, makes it an ideal destination for a day's excursion.

With its attractive mountain setting, picturesque little streets and whitewashed houses, Mijas is a popular excursion from the coast.

On the central square of Plaza de la Virgen you will see the ever-patient donkeys lined up. Adorned with colourful saddles and tassles, they can be hired for rides around town, serving as donkey taxis. Concerts and fiestas are sometimes held in the square, which centres around a small fountain and is a popular meeting place. Below is a large parking lot, which has greatly helped to ease traffic problems.

Adjoining the square is a neat little park with fine views. Hollowed out from a chunk of rock is a delightful little chapel known as the Santuario de la Virgen de la Peña Limosnas.

Inside is the image of Santa Maria de la Peña, along with some impressive candlesticks, embroidered garments and other religious relics.

A stroll to the Plaza de la Constitución leads past the Miniature Museum 'Carromato de Max', which has a collection of tiny curios. Up the slope from the Plaza stands the charming little parish church of La Inmaculada Concepción, built mostly in the Mozarabic style. Near by is the town's small, rectangular bullring.

37km west of Málaga · Local bus services · Benalmádena Pueblo (➤ 87) · St Anthony's Day (16–17 Jan); Feria de la Virgen de la Peña (early Sep); Romería de Santa Teresa (end Oct) · Tourist information: Ayuntamiento, Plaza Virgen de la Peña s/n · 952 48 59 00

Puente Nuevo Ronda

The old town of Ronda is famed for its spectacular setting and views of the bridge over the El Tajo ravine.

Ronda has long associations with painters and writers, for many of whom the town has held a deep fascination. The scene of Ronda perched on the clifftop and, in particular, the bridge which spans the gorge, has been the subject of countless paintings and photographs.

Ronda is one of Spain's oldest cities. Situated within the rugged landscape of the Serranía de Ronda, the town is split in two, divided by the gorge of the River Guadalevín, which is spanned by the Puente Nuevo (New Bridge). The dramatic views from the bridge, combined with the attractions of the old town and its historical interest, make Ronda (► 130) a top excursion for visitors staying along the coast.

The Puente Nuevo (which has become the city's symbol) was begun in 1751 and completed in 1793. It stands a full 96m above the Tajo Gorge at its highest and narrowest point. The unfortunate architect fell to his death from a basket lowered to allow him to inspect the building work.

✉ 118km northwest of Málaga 🚌 Buses from Algeciras, Cádiz, Málaga (via Torremolinos, Marbella, San Pedro) and Servilla ↔ Ronda (► 130), Cuevas de la Pileta (► 133) ℹ Ronda (► 130)

Puerto Banús

The dazzling marina of Puerto Banús, with its luxurious yachts, trendy restaurants and bars, serves as a magnet for visitors to the Costa del Sol.

A stay on the Costa del Sol would be incomplete without a visit to Puerto Banús, one of the Costa's most famous attractions. Built in 1968, Puerto José Banús, as it is also known, was the creation of promoter José Banús and was one of Spain's first village-type harbour developments. The result is most attractive and worth a visit.

Backed by the mountains, a ring of brilliant white apartment houses surrounds the marina, which is filled with craft of all sizes, from mega-yachts to small sailing boats. A feature of Banús is the Arab-built complex of luxury apartments, located on the right as you enter the port. With its opulent marble façade and gleaming turrets, the inspiration could have been taken straight from the *Arabian Nights*.

Around the port is a string of cafés, bars and restaurants, along with boutiques and gift shops. While frontline restaurants are *the* places in which to be seen, better value is sometimes found in some of the small restaurants in the streets behind, tucked away up flights of stairs. In season the quayside is thronged with people who come to see, or to be seen – this can be a great place for celebrity-spotting. The Saladuba Pub and the Frank Sinatra Bar are favourite haunts for indulging this particular pastime.

At night the place becomes a hive of activity, as the smart restaurants, trendy piano bars and clubs fill up with beautiful people. While the glamour of its earlier days may have dimmed, Banús still rates as a star attraction.

64km west of Málaga, 6km west of Marbella · Bus services from Marbella and San Pedro de Alcántara · San Pedro de Alcántara (► 138) · Regattas, sailing and fishing competitions · Tourist Information: Avenida Principal s/n · 952 11 38 30 (summer only)

Málaga

Málaga is the second city of Andalucía and capital of the Costa del Sol, forming a natural divide between its western and eastern sections. The town has an attractive setting, crowned by the old Moorish castle which stands atop the Gibralfaro Hill, holding a commanding view of Málaga's harbour and the wide sweep of the bay.

The backing of the Montes de Málaga mountain range provides shelter from the wind, ensuring a pleasant Mediterranean climate which is particularly agreeable from autumn through to spring.

To many tourists Málaga has tended to serve primarily as a gateway to the coast or its hinterland. Now, with the opening of the Picasso Museum, along with several other new museums and expansion projects, there is an awakening of interest in the city whose old quarters, churches, traditional bars and restaurants exude a true flavour of Andalucía.

MÁLAGA

Málaga has, by and large, retained its own personality over the years, remaining relatively untouched by the tourist boom along the coast.

It is well worth spending some time to explore the town. Off the Alameda Principal, Málaga's main avenue, attractively shaded by palms and lined with flower stalls and kiosks, is the old town. Here you will find yourself in another world of narrow streets with traditional bars and bodegas exuding a decidedly local flavour.

Málaga's outstanding features are the old Moorish Alcazaba (fortress) (➤ 16) and the Castillo de Gibralfaro (➤ 48), which offer magnificent views of the town and the bay. Other attractions include the cathedral, the Museo Picasso, the Museo de Artes y Costumbres Populares and the Palacio de la Aduana. Among the many small churches in Malaga don't miss the chapel of the Santuario de la Victoria. For good seafood restaurants head for the beach suburbs of El Palo or Pedregalejo.

A good way to visit the town is by the electric train which runs half hourly between Fuengirola and Málaga, making stops at Torremolinos and other centres en route.

Tourist information: Pasaje de Chinitas 4 ☎ 952 21 34 45

DISCOVER MÁLAGA

CASA NATAL DE PICASSO

Spain's celebrated painter, Pablo Ruiz Picasso, was born in 1881 in the corner house of an elegant yellow-toned block on Plaza de la Merced. His birthplace was declared an historic artistic monument in 1983, and in 1991 it became the headquarters of the Pablo Ruiz Picasso Foundation. The centre has been created to foster cultural activities, including the promotion of contemporary art with a special emphasis on Picasso himself.

Visitors are welcome to take a look around the small area on the first floor where you can see a few photographs, memorabilia and documentation relating to Picasso's life, in addition to works by other artists.

It was here that Picasso began to paint, helped by his father, an art teacher, who had recognised his young son's talent.

✉ Plaza de la Merced 15 ☎ 952 06 02 15 🕑 Mon–Sat 10–8, Sun 10–2 ✋ Free 🚉 Centro-Alameda railway station

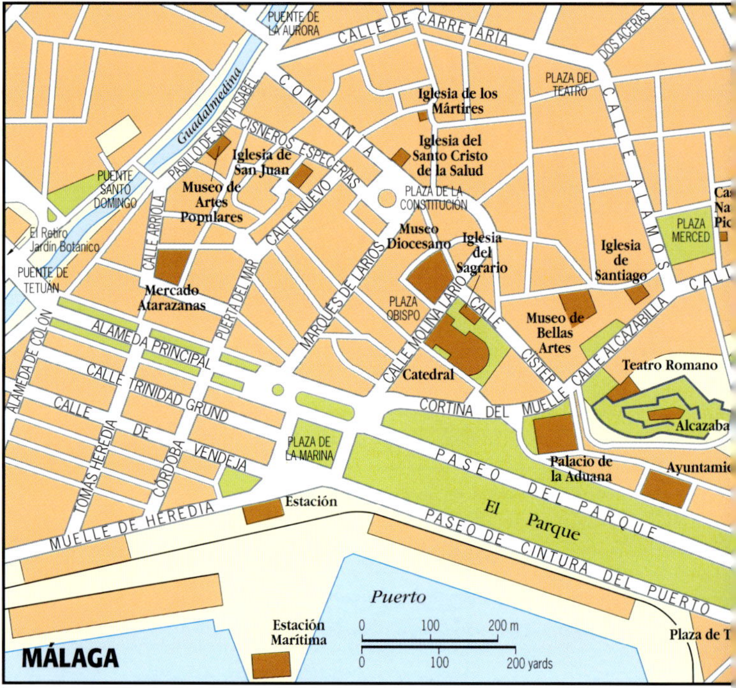
MÁLAGA
PUENTE DE LA AURORA
CALLE DE CARRETERÍA
DOS ACERAS
PLAZA DEL TEATRO
CALLE ÁLAMOS
COMPAÑÍA
Guadalmedina
PASILLO DE SANTA ISABEL
CISNEROS
ESPECERÍAS
Iglesia de los Mártires
Iglesia del Santo Cristo de la Salud
Iglesia de San Juan
Museo de Artes Populares
PUENTE SANTO DOMINGO
CALLE NUEVO
PLAZA DE LA CONSTITUCIÓN
PLAZA MERCED
El Retiro Jardín Botánico
CALLE ARRIOLA
Museo Diocesano
Iglesia del Sagrario
Iglesia de Santiago
PUENTE DE TETUÁN
Mercado Atarazanas
PUERTA DEL MAR
MARQUÉS DE LARIOS
PLAZA OBISPO
CALLE MOLINA LARIO
CALLE CISTER
Museo de Bellas Artes
CALLE ALCAZABILLA
ALAMEDA DE COLÓN
ALAMEDA PRINCIPAL
CALLE TRINIDAD GRUND
Catedral
Teatro Romano
CALLE DE VENDEJA
TOMÁS HEREDIA
CÓRDOBA
CORTINA DEL MUELLE
Alcazaba
PLAZA DE LA MARINA
PASEO DEL PARQUE
Palacio de la Aduana
Ayuntamie
Estación
El Parque
MUELLE DE HEREDIA
PASEO DE CINTURA DEL PUERTO
Puerto
Estación Marítima
0
100
200 m
200 yards
Plaza de T

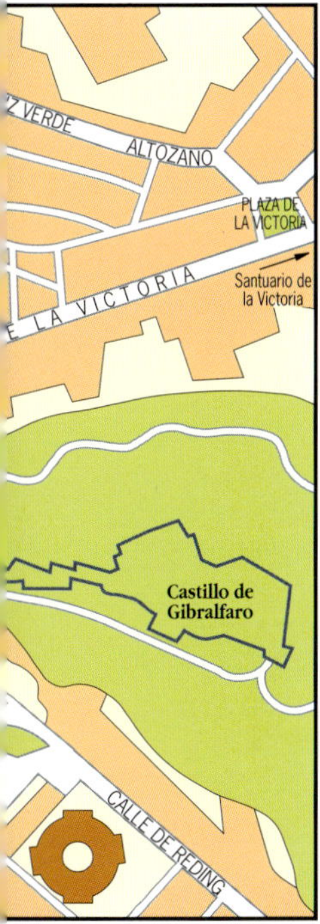

Málaga's cathedral

CASTILLO DE GIBRALFARO

Right above the Alcazaba stands the Castillo de Gibralfaro, crowning the hill of the same name. It was built by Yusef I of Granada at the beginning of the 14th century on a formerly Phoenician site and lighthouse from which its name was derived – *gebel-faro* (rock of the lighthouse) signifies the beacon that served to guide ships into the harbour.

This was the scene of a three-month siege by the citizens of Málaga against the Catholic Monarchs Ferdinand and Isabella. The matter was concluded when hunger led to capitulation, after which Ferdinand occupied the site while his queen took up residence in the town. All that remains today of this historic monument are the solid ramparts which rise among dense woods of pines and eucalyptus, with the Alcazaba below.

Although it can be reached on foot from the Alcazaba, it's a safer bet to visit the castle direct, by bus, car, even by horse and carriage. You can round off a visit with a cool drink at the nearby Parador de Málaga which also offers views of the city and harbour.

Lighthouse Hill 952 22 72 30 Daily 9–6 Inexpensive
Parador near by 35

CATEDRAL

Málaga's cathedral was built between 1528 and 1782 on or near the site of a former mosque. While original plans had allowed for two towers, lack of funds resulted in the completion of only one, giving rise to the name by which the cathedral is affectionately referred – La Manquita – loosely interpreted as 'the little one-armed woman'.

The interior has influences of Renaissance and baroque styles. The notable 17th-century choir stalls of mahogany and cedarwood were designed by Luis Ortíz. After his death the 40 finely carved statues of the saints behind each stall were completed by Pedro de Mena, one of Spain's most celebrated wood-carvers of the time, who spent some years in Málaga.

Adjoining the cathedral is the Iglesia del Sagrario. Founded in the 15th century on the site of a mosque, the church has an unusual rectangular shape. Its Isabelline-Gothic portal is the only remaining part of the original structure, which was rebuilt in 1714. The interior is richly decorated and its main altar features a magnificent 16th-century retable.

Calle Molina Larios, s/n 952 21 59 17 Mon–Sat 10–6:45
Inexpensive Centro-Alameda railway station

walk

This walk starts in the Plaza de la Marina and makes a tour of the old quarters, taking in the cathedral and several churches.

From Plaza de la Marina take Calle Molina Lario, left of the Málaga Palacio Hotel which faces you. A few moments' walk will bring you right up to the cathedral.

Horses and carriages line up here ready to take visitors on a tour around the town. Opposite, on the Plaza Obispo, is the old Palacio Episcopal which holds exhibitions of contemporary art.

Turn right along Calle Santa Maria and take Calle San Agustín.

On your right is the Palacio Buenavista, which now houses the new Museo Picasso. You will now enter an attractive section of pedestrianised streets and pretty coloured houses.

The statue of Santa Maria de la Victoria in Málaga's cathedral

Fork right into Calle Granada which takes you by the Iglesia de Santiago. Continue to the Plaza de la Merced.

The centre of the Plaza de la Merced is marked by an obelisk in memory of General Torrijos and his men who were shot after the War of Independence. On the far corner, in a block of houses, is the Casa Natal de Picasso, birthplace of Pablo Picasso, now centre of the Picasso Foundation.

Return down Calle Granada to Plaza del Siglo and on to the Plaza de la Constitucíon, then stroll down Calle Marqués Larios, Málaga's main shopping street. Down on the left make a short detour through the archway and along Pasaje de Chinitas, which leads to a tiny square. Complete the walk down Calle Larios and turn into the Alameda Principal to Plaza de la Marina.

Distance 4km **Time** 3–4 hours, depending on visits to churches
Start/end point Plaza de la Marina **Lunch** Espartero (€€)
✉ Esparteros 4 ☎ 952 60 30 22

CENTRO (CENTRE)

The heart of Málaga is found north of the Alameda Principal, Málaga's main avenue, and east of the Río Guadalmedina, which separates the old town from the new. As soon as you turn off the Alameda you will enter a labyrinthine medieval world of narrow, twisting roads. There is much to be enjoyed here, increasingly so the more you find your bearings. The centre is small and many streets are pedestrianised, so that exploring on foot is both enjoyable and viable.

Another way in which to enjoy a tour around town is by horse-drawn carriage. You will find these by the cathedral, in the Paseo del Parque and other points around the town.

While the cathedral is a focal point from which to start exploring, the main artery of the city centre is the busy shopping street, Calle Marqués de Larios, which leads from the Alameda Principal north to the Plaza de la Constitución. On either side are old, narrow streets, alleyways and tiny squares where you can happily browse for hours. Within this area are a number of churches and a few museums. You will also discover some delightfully picturesque little streets lined with gaily coloured houses and shops.

IGLESIAS (CHURCHES)

When strolling around Málaga's old town, you are more than likely to pass by several, if not all, of the following churches. Take time to have a look inside, as each has its own individual attraction. With the exception of the Santuario de la Victoria, which is slightly away from the centre, all are within easy walking distance of each other.

CATEDRAL **(➤ 49)**

Iglesia de los Mártires

IGLESIA DE LOS MÁRTIRES

The church was founded in 1487 by the Catholic Monarchs and dedicated to the martyrs of the town. It features a striking Mudéjar tower which was added later and a richly decorated baroque-style interior, which includes a notable sculpture by Francisco Ortíz of Jesus praying on the Mount of Olives.

Plaza Mártires · 952 21 27 24 · Daily 10–2:30, 6–7:30 · Free

IGLESIA DE SANTIAGO

Founded in 1490, the church is noted for its tall, Mudéjar-style steeple and baroque interior which contains some notable chapels. Pablo Picasso's baptismal certificate is stored here.

Calle Granada 62 · 952 21 03 99 · Daily 9–1:30, 6–9

IGLESIA DEL SANTO CRISTO DE LA SALUD

The interior of this 17th-century church is a real gem. Note the brilliant altarpiece and beautifully decorated cupola. The church also contains the tomb of architect Pedro de la Mena.

✉ Calle Compania ☎ 952 21 34 56

IGLESIA SAN JUAN BAUTISTA

Founded in 1490, the church's baroque-style tower above the main entrance was added in 1770. Inside are several fine chapels and a rich altarpiece. The 17th-century figure of San Juan is the work of Francisco Ortíz.

✉ Calle San Juan, 3 ☎ 952 21 12 83 🕒 Daily 8:30–1, 6–8

SANTUARIO DE LA VICTORIA

The church was erected in 1487 on the site where the Catholic Monarchs pitched their tents during the siege of that year. A major feature is the magnificent retable which rises above the main altar. High up, amidst a flourish of exuberant ornamentation, is a small *camerín* (chapel) containing a statue of the Madonna and Child (reached by stairs at the far end of the church). In the crypt is the family vault of the counts of Buenavista, who were responsible for the rebuilding of the church in the 17th century.

Plaza del Santuario 952 25 26 47 Tue–Fri 10–12, 4:30–7, Sat 10–12 Free Centro-Alameda railway station

MUSEO PICASSO

The new Picasso Museum is installed in the Palacio Buenavista, former home of the Palace of Fine Arts. The museum contains over 180 works by the artist, including drawings, engravings, lithographs, sculptures and ceramics, the majority of which have been donated by Christina, Picasso's daughter-in-law. Work continues to extend the premises and restore the façade. The museum opened in 2003.

Palacio de Buenavista, Calle San Augustin, 8 902 44 33 77 Tue–Thu 10–8, Fri and Sat 10–1:30 Moderate Wheelchairs available upon request

MUSEO DE ARTES Y COSTUMBRES POPULARES

This charming little museum is housed in the Mesón de la Victoria, a former 17th-century inn, now attractively restored. The museum is on two floors and was created to give an insight into the past ways and customs of the people of the region.

The first rooms, which display agricultural items, open out onto an attractive courtyard with tropical plants. In the rooms beyond you can see a fishing boat and some interiors of old houses. Upstairs displays include collections of costumes, ceramics and tiles, fascinating old posters announcing fiestas, religious items and an enchanting little group of clay figures depicting a *panda de verdiales* (group of regional musicians).

✉ Passillo de Santa Isabel 10 ☎ 952 21 71 37 ⌚ Mon–Sat 10–1, 5–7
Inexpensive Railway station Centro-Alameda

PARQUES Y JARDINES (PARKS & GARDENS)

In and around Málaga are several attractive parks and gardens, of which the following are outstanding.

EL PARQUE

Malaga's city park, which runs alongside the Paseo del Parque, was created at the end of the 19th century making use of land reclaimed from the sea. The park contains beautiful tropical flowering trees and shrubs. Many of the unusual and exotic species to be seen here were brought from overseas when Málaga was an important world trading centre.

✉ Between Paseo del Parque and Paseo de Espana ☎ None
🕐 Daily ✋ Free ♿ Good

EL RETIRO JARDÍN BOTÁNICO-ORNITOLÓGICO

The El Retiro is an old botanic garden and bird sanctuary, where monks once came to find peace and to meditate. Recently opened to the public, its ornithological park contains hundreds of birds, many of them endangered species. A peaceful stroll can be enjoyed amongst its trees, ponds and fountains.

✉ Ctra de Coín ☎ 952 62 16 00 ⏲ Daily 9–6 ✋ Moderate
🍴 Restaurant (€€)

JARDÍN BOTÁNICO-HISTÓRICO 'LA CONCEPCIÓN'

Just outside Málaga, Finca de la Concepción is another magnificent botanic garden. You can follow a marked path through exotic trees and plants, passing Roman sculpture and a waterfall.

✉ Along the N331 to Antequera, just off the Málaga ring road
☎ 952 25 21 48 ⏲ Tue–Sun 10–4:30 ✋ Inexpensive

walk

This is a leisurely walk which includes Málaga's main market, an attractive little museum and several churches.

From the Centro-Alameda take the Alameda Principal exit. Cross over at the traffic lights and turn into Calle Torregarda to the Mercado de Atarazas, Malaga's main market.

Pass through the market to look at the displays of fruit and vegetables and the glistening fresh fish.

Emerge into Plaza de Arriola and continue along the Paseo Santa Isabel.

The tiny courtyard of the Museo de Artes Populares

You will find yourself on the banks of the dried up Río Guadalmedina. Look out for a flight of steps on your right which leads down through a garden to the Museo de Artes Populares.

Continue along the Paseo Santa Isabel and turn right down Calle Cisneros.

This brings you into a picturesque part of the old town where a right turn down a narrow alleyway leads to the Iglesia San Juan, standing on a small square.

Retrace your steps, turn right onto Calle Especerías, left along Calle Salvago, left then right to Plaza San Ignacio.

Take a look at the Iglesia del Corazón de Jesús. Turn back and take the Calle de los Mártires. On the small square which follows, you cannot miss the striking Mudéjar tower of the Iglesia de los Mártires.

Return and turn left along Calle Compañia, past the Iglesia de Santo Cristo de la Salud.

Wander through the Plaza de la Constitución and take the Calle Nueva into the heart of Malaga's famous area for tapas bars. The Calle Puerta del Mar leads straight down to the Alameda Principal and back to the station.

Distance 3.5km **Time** 3–4 hours, depending on visits
Start/end point Railway station Centro-Alameda 1
Lunch Mesón la Aldea (€) ✉ Esparteros, 5 ☎ 952 22 76 89

Where to eat & drink... Málaga

ADOLFO (€€)

Good-quality restaurant known for its excellent local and international cuisine.

✉ Paseo Marítimo Pablo Ruiz Picasso 12 ☎ 952 60 19 14 🕑 Lunch and dinner, closed Sun

ANTONIO MARTÍN (€€€)

Seafront restaurant with large terrace. A long-time favourite, specialising in seafood.

✉ Paseo Marítimo ☎ 952 22 73 98 🕑 Lunch and dinner, closed Sun dinner

LA CANCELA (€)

Two small dining rooms. Specialities include *fritura malagueña* and *ajo blanco*.

✉ Calle Denis Belgrano 3 ☎ 952 22 31 25 🕑 Lunch and dinner, closed Wed evening

CASA DEL GUARDIA (€)

One of Málaga's oldest bars, lined with barrels. A good place to sample sweet wines and great variety of *tapas*.

✉ Alameda Principal ☎ None 🕐 Lunch and dinner

CASA PEDRO (€€)

Long-standing favourite with the locals. Large dining area overlooking the sea.

✉ Quitapenas 121, El Palo beach ☎ 952 29 00 13 🕐 Lunch and dinner, closed Mon dinner

EL CHINITAS (€€)

Lively, known for its good *tapas*. Specialises in Andalucían and Mediterranean dishes. Commemorative plaques to García Lorca outside.

✉ Calle Moreno Monroy 4–6 ☎ 952 21 0972 🕐 Lunch and dinner

LA ESPUELA (€€)

Good local dishes in cosy, Andalucían atmosphere.

✉ Obispo Herrara Oria 5 ☎ 952 28 11 98 🕐 Lunch and dinner, closed Sun

EL FIGÓN DE BONILLA (€€)

Known for its good local cooking and fish dishes.

✉ Calle Cervantes ☎ 952 22 32 23 🕐 Lunch and dinner, closed Sun

LO GÜENO (€)

Typical *tapas* bar offering a wide choice.

✉ Calle Marín García 9 ☎ 952 22 21 80 🕐 Lunch and dinner

MESÓN ASTORGA (€€)

Known for its traditional Andalucían cooking.

✉ Calle Gerona 11 ☎ 952 34 25 63 🕐 Lunch and dinner, closed Wed

ORELLANA (€)

Great favourite with Malagueñians. The speciality here is stuffed squid.

✉ Calle Moreno Moreno 5 ☎ 952 23 30 12 🕐 Lunch and dinner

REFECTORIUM (€€€)

Traditional restaurant specialising in meat dishes.

✉ Calle Cervantes, 8 ☎ 952 21 89 90 🕐 Lunch and dinner

Where to stay...
Málaga

DON CURRO (€€)

Medium-range hotel, conveniently positioned between the old town and the seafront. Within easy walking distance of Málaga's major attractions.

✉ Sancha Lara 7 ☎ 952 22 72 00

LOS NARANJOS (€€)

In residential district, near the centre. Small garden with orange trees.

✉ Paseo Sancha, 35 ☎ 952 22 43 17

PARADOR MÁLAGA-GIBRALFARO (€€)

High up the hill by Gibralfaro Castle with magnificent views of Málaga and bay.

✉ Gibralfaro ☎ 952 22 19 02

HOTEL GRADINGS

Officially registered hotels in Spain range from 1 to 5 star (with an additional top deluxe category of GL, Gran Lujo). Other types of accommodation include apartment hotels, hotel residencias (no restaurant), hostels and pensions. Stars are assigned according to services and facilities available. Suites can usually be found in the 4- or 5-star range. Tariffs should be displayed.

PARADORES

Very pleasant accommodation is provided by the *parador*, originally denoting a lodging place for the gentry. The late 1920s saw the development of this network of state-run establishments. Often in attractively converted old castles and historic buildings, paradores are scattered throughout the country, making good stopovers when touring by car. There are also some purpose-built modern paradores in tourist centres, many set in tranquil gardens, often with a pool, in lovely surroundings. Although tariffs have risen over the years, the splendour of the buildings and their locations make an overnight stay well worthwhile.

RURAL RETREATS

As a total contrast to the beach, visitors may like to venture into Andalucía's hinterland. At a short distance from the coast are to be found a number of so-called rural lodgings, which can vary from country cottages, rooms in attractive *haciendas* to mountain refuges or hostels and facilities for camping. In addition to wonderful scenery and fresh mountain air, there are often possibilities for hiking, riding and other pursuits. Information and reservation centre:

RAAR (Red Andaluza de Alojamientos Rurales)

✉ Apdo. 2035, 04080 Almeria ☎ 902 44 22 33; fax 950 27 16 78; www.raar.es

You can also contact:

AHRA (Asocación de Hoteles Rurales de Andalucía)

✉ Centro Cultural Hospital de Santiago, Calle Cristo Rey 2, 23400 Ubeda (Jaén) ☎ 953 75 58 67

Rural Andalus

✉ Calle Don Cristián 10, 29007 Málaga ☎ 952 27 62 29; fax 952 27 65 567; www.ruralandalus.es

Costa del Sol & beyond

The Costa del Sol falls into two parts with Málaga forming the divide between the western and eastern sections. The most developed and best known area is west of Málaga, starting with Torremolinos and including the major resorts of Benalmádena Costa, Fuengirola, Marbella and Estepona. This part of the coastline is virtually one long stream of apartment blocks, marina developments, hotels and restaurants.

The eastern Costa del Sol, stretching towards Almería, has a totally different appeal. The coastline is often broken up by rocks and small coves and is much less developed, with Nerja standing out as a favoured resort. The interior offers excursions to delighful white Andalucían villages nestling in the mountains, and to the great historic cities of Granada, Córdoba and Sevilla.

Alameda
Corbones
Sierra de Yeguas
Mollina
Las Rozas
El Saucejo
Laguna de la Fuente de Piedra
Villanueva de San Juan
Campillos
Antequera
Embalse de Guadalhorce
Almargen
Teba
Sierra de Chimenea
Olvera
Cañete la Real
Embalse del Chorro
Garganta del Chorro
Parque Natural Torcal de Antequera
Setenil
Ardales
Casaberme
Embalse de Zahara
Carratraca
Álora
El Burgo
Grazalema
Guadalhorce
Pizarra
Finca de la Concepció
Tajo de Ronda
Cueva del Hundimiento
Ronda
Serranía de Ronda
Yunquera
Alozaina
MÁLAGA
Cueva del Gato
Cártama
Cueva de la Pileta
1918m
Tolox
Coín
Alhaurín el Grande
Torremolinos
Benalmádena
Arroyo de la Miel
Istán
Castillo de Agulla
Jubrique
Mijas
Benalmádena Costa
Gaucín
Ojén
Sierra Bermeja
Benahavís
Marbella
Fuengirola
Genal
Puerto Banús
1449m
Calahonda
San Pedro de Alcántara
Casares
Estepona

Embalse de Iznájar
Huétor-Taja
Loja
Fuente Vaqueros
Genil
Santafé
Granada
La Alhambra
Mala
Cacín
Albama
chidona
Sierra de Loja
Santa Cruz de Alhama
Puerto del Suspiro del Moro 860m
Alhama de Granada
a de Camorolos
Padul
Sierra Nevada
Embalse de los Bermejales
Zafarraya
Dúrcal
Arenas del Rey
Periana
Sierra de Tejeda
2065m
Órjiva
Colmenar
Dúrcal
Sierra del Chaparral
Sierra de Almijara
Otívar
Vélez de Benaudalla
Competa
Málaga
Vélez-Málaga
Frigiliana
Benamocarra
Torrox
Cuevas de Nerja
Salobreña
Motril
Nerja
Torre del Mar
Torrox Costa
Almuñécar
Calahonda
va del uerón
Rincón de la Victoria
Cabo Sacratif
0
10
20
30 km
0
10
20 miles
COSTA DEL SOL

ALMUÑÉCAR

Almuñécar, situated in the province of Granada, within the coastline now designated as the Costa Tropical, lies amidst orchards of tropical fruits. It presents a very picturesque scene, typical of so many villages to be found in southern Spain, with a cluster of whitewashed houses rising up the hillside, crowned by an old castle. Its history goes back to the time of the Phoenicians, with subsequent occupation by the Romans and the Moors.

The Castillo de San Miguel stands on top of a tall rock, dividing two bays. It was built during the reign of Carlos V, over the site of a former Moorish fortress, and features a great square tower known as La Mazmorra.

The town itself is a delightful jumble of narrow, cobblestoned streets, climbing steeply up to the summit.

Don't miss a visit to the Ornithological Park located at the foot of the hill. Here you can see brilliantly coloured parrots and rare species of birds in a beautiful setting of subtropical plants and flowers. The seafront is lined with apartment blocks, bars and restaurants, with a lively scene by day and night, during the season.

Also worth a visit is the small archaeological museum housed in the Cueva de los Siete Palacios, thought to have been a Roman reservoir for water. The museum has a display of local artefacts (Tue–Sat 11–2 and 6–8).

A look-out post at nearby Punta de la Mona offers sweeping views of the harbour and the Mediterranean.

84km east of Málaga Local bus services Tourist Information: Avenida Europa-Palacete La Najarra 958 63 11 25

ANTEQUERA

Antequera is known for its convents, churches and elegant mansions, which show various architectural influences. It is easily reached by means of the good motorway from Málaga and can be visited in a day. (town walk ➤ 84–85 and Drive from Torremolinos ➤ 158–159).

The town is dominated by the old castle, from where there are excellent views of the surrounding plains. The 16th-century church of Santa María la Mayor, near by, features a fine Mudéjar ceiling. Dominant are the bell towers of the churches of San Sebastian and San Augustín, which combine the Mudéjar and baroque styles. The church of El Carmen, a designated national monument and former convent, it is noted for its rich interior and impressive wooden altar.

The discovery of prehistoric tombs in nearby caves has given the town added prominence. Of the three caves here, the most important is the **Dólmen de Menga**. Its large cavern contains a series of stones and columns which support huge slabs that form the roof, believed to date back to circa 2500BC.

The Parque Nacional El Torcal de Antequera is located some 16km south of Antequera and covers an extended area of grey limestone rocks and boulders which have been weathered with time to form the most weird and wonderful shapes. There is a small information office by the car park and a magnificent view from the nearby Mirador el Ventanillo. Several walking trails among the boulders are marked by arrows (yellow for a shorter walk, red for a longer one).

✉ 54km north of Málaga 🚌 From Málaga 🚆 From Málaga
? Fería de Primavera (31 May–1/2 Jun); Noche Flamenca de Santa Maria (end Jul); August Fair (early Aug) ℹ Tourist Information: Plaza San Sebastian 7 ☎ 952 70 25 05

Dólmen de Menga
✉ 1km east of Antequera 🕐 Wed–Sat 9–6, Tue, Sun 9–3:30 ✋ Free
🚌 From Antequera 🚆 From Antequera ♿ None

walk

This walk takes in some of Antequera's many churches and includes magnificent views. Most churches close from 1:30 to 4pm so a morning walk is recommended. On the Plaza San Sebastian look at the 16th-century Colegiata de San Sebastian. Walk up Calle Infante Don Fernando. Take a look at the Iglesia de San Agustín, on the left, and further along, on the right, you will pass the Palacio Consistorial (Town Hall) and the Convento de los Remedios.

Just past the Iglesia de San Juan de Dios turn sharp right into Calle Cantareros and back towards the centre.

You will pass the house of the Condado de Colchado and the Convento de la Madre de Dios de Monteagudo.

Continue down Calle Diego Ponce, then turn left up to Plaza San Francisco and the Plazuela de San Zoilo.

This brings you to the Convento Real de San Zoilo, one of Antequera's National Monuments, and fine views.

Take Calle Calzada and continue up Cuesta de Los Rojos to Plaza del Carmen. On Calle del Carmen is the Iglesia del Carmen. Return and take a sharp right, turn up Calle del Colegio, a very steep climb, to the Arco de los Gigantes (Arch of Giants) on your left.

Pass through the arch to the Real Colegiata de Santa Maria la Mayor. Near by are the Roman Baths.

Return through the Arch and go left along Calle Herradores to the charming Plaza del Portichuelo on which stands the Iglesia de Santa Maria de Jesús.

Distance 4.5km **Time** About 3 hours **Start point** Plaza San Sebastian **End point** Plaza del Portichuelo **Lunch** Restaurante El Angelote (€€) ✉ Calle Encarnación (Esquina Cosa Viejo) ☎ 952 70 34 65

BENALMÁDENA COSTA

Benalmádena Costa is, in effect, a natural extension of Torremolinos, taking over where Torremolinos leaves off. It covers a long stretch of coast lined with the type of high-rise apartment blocks which characterise this section of the Costa del Sol, along with a string of restaurants, cafés, bars and shops. An attractive seafront promenade makes it possible to walk from Torremolinos all the way along the coast to Benalmádena's Puerto Marina (► 90–91) – you need time and energy for this!

The area has been noticeably upgraded in recent years, partly due to the casino and the 18-hole Torrequebrada golf course, located a short distance up into the hills. There are also facilities for waterskiing, jetskiing, windsurfing, sailing and all the popular watersports.

✉ 20km west of Málaga 🚌 Connections 🚆 Railway station Benalmádena–Arroyo de la Miel ⇔ Sea Life Centre (► 223) ? Virgen del Carmen fiesta (16 Jul) ℹ Avenida Antonio Machado 10 ☎ 952 44 12 95; www.benalmadena.com

BENALMÁDENA PUEBLO

Two small inland communities present a complete contrast to the attractions on the coastal strip of Benalmádena Costa. About 1km into the hills is Arroyo de la Miel which has developed into quite a lively centre with modern housing, shops and restaurants. Just up the road is the Tivoli World Show and Amusement Park.

Farther up the hill is Benalmádena Pueblo whose origins are thought to date back to Phoenician times. This is a charming little village of narrow twisting streets and whitewashed houses. With attractive views of the coast and surrounding landscapes, it offers a rural atmosphere. The Museo Arqueológico contains some pre-Columbian exhibits, along with artefacts from Roman and early Iberian times.

☒ 3km west of Arroyo de la Miel ? Local fair (15 Aug); Fería de San Juan (24 Jun) at Arroyo de la Miel

drive

This drive takes you up into the hills through attractive scenery to the picturesque little town of Mijas, passing a couple of other typical Andalucían villages on the return to the coast.

From Benalmádena Costa take the N340 east for a short distance. Turn inland, following the sign to Arroyo de la Miel. In the village turn left at the traffic lights and follow the signs to Tivoli World. Continue up the hill and pass by the Tivoli World Amusement Park on your right to Benalmádena Pueblo. Proceed through the village and follow the signs to Mijas.

A very winding road (with some bad stretches and narrow sections) takes you through lovely pine-clad hillls, with fine views down to the coast. You should reach Mijas some 45 minutes later. Take time to explore this delightful little town, noted for its setting in the hills.

Take the A387 northwest to Alhaurín el Grande, 17km on.

Drive on with some fine panoramic views on your left and bear right, continuing on the A387, to the village of Alhaurín el Grande. Look for the signs and join the A366 northwest to Coín, which you should reach some 10 minutes later.

After Coín, turn onto the A355, following the signs for Ojén-Marbella, to Monda. Continue on the A355 which now heads south towards Ojén-Marbella.

The road from here to Ojén has a good surface and continuing curves as it passes through an area of rocks and wooded hills. It will take you some 45 minutes to reach Ojén.

Continue south for 8km to the coastal road. Join the N340 and take direction Málaga back to Benalmádena Costa.

Distance 116km **Time** About 5 hours, allowing time to visit Mijas **Start/end point** Banalmádena Costa **Lunch** Restaurante Mesón El Olivar (€€) ✉ Avenida Virgen de la Pena (edif. El Roasrio) ☎ 952 48 61 96 🕑 Closed Sat and Feb

RESTAURANTE
EL MERO
PIZZERIA
Restaurante
PASEOS:
POR EL PUERTO

BENALMÁDENA PUERTO MARINA

Benalmádena's Puerto Marina, or Puerto Departivo as it is known, has developed into one of the most prominent of the marinas which have sprung up along the coast.

Initially a small harbour surrounded by whitewashed houses, Andalucian-style, it has gradually grown into an impressive marina, with more than 1,000 berths. Shops, open-air bars and restaurants line the quayside. The centrepiece is provided by a complex of luxurious apartments called Las Islas de Puerto Marina. Constructed in flamboyant style, they appear to be islands floating on the water. An outstanding attraction here is Sea Life Benalmádena (► 223), while another popular venue is the *Willow*, the Mississippi-style paddleboat; moored here permanently, it is now a restaurant and nightclub.

With its open-air cafés, restaurants and shops, Puerto Marina continues to increase in popularity, especially at weekends, attracting locals and visitors alike with further expansion planned. An ultramodern underwater lighting system, installed in the waters of the harbour, creates a magical effect at night.

☒ Benalmádena Costa ⇔ Torrequebrada development with casino, nightclub and golf course

CASARES (➤ 21)

(➤ 21)

CÓMPETA

Way up in the mountains of La Axarquia, the region east of Málaga, is the small town of Cómpeta, which can be reached by taking the road leading inland from Torox-Costa.

Cómpeta is noted for its attractive setting, perched atop a mountain ridge surrounded by vineyards. It is one of a number of easily accessible Andalucían towns and villages located in the hills which offer fine views down to the coast. The town is made up of a cluster of whitewashed houses and winding streets. On the main square stands the baroque Iglesia de la Asunción, which features an impressive bell tower.

Cómpeta has quite a sizeable community of foreign residents, a number of whom are involved with craft industries. A big attraction is the lively wine festival which is held each year in August in the main square.

51km east of Málaga · Local services · Nerja (➤ 127)
Noche del Vino (15 Aug) · Tourist information: Plaza Almijira s/n
952 55 33 01

CÓRDOBA

Córdoba is one of Andalucía's richest jewels. In addition to the Mezquita or Great Mosque (➤ 26–28), the city's old quarter of narrow streets with flower-filled balconies and patios allows visitors an insight into the essence of southern Spain. The town lies along the banks of the River Guadalquivir, overlooked by the Sierra de Córdoba. With extremes of heat in the summer and harsh winters, good times to visit are spring or autumn.

Tools found on the banks of the River Guadalquivir suggest that palaeolithic man lived here. Córdoba later became a leading centre of the people of Tartessos and was then conquered by the Carthaginians, the Romans (when it became the capital of Baetica) and the Moors.

In 929, under Moorish rule, the Caliphate of Córdoba was established. With the founding of a university, Córdoba became a renowned centre of art, culture and learning. This period saw the construction of Córdoba's great Mezquita and other fine examples of Moorish architecture.

Gradually, in the 11th and 12th centuries, Córdoba went into decline. With the breaking up of the Caliphate into small *tarifas* (states), Córdoba came under the jurisdiction of Sevilla. After it fell to the Christians in 1236, the Catholic Monarchs presided here while planning the reconquest of Granada and it was here that Queen Isabella granted Columbus the commission for his voyage of discovery.

The city has many attractions and should be explored on foot. Bear in mind that some of its narrow streets do not easily accommodate pedestrians and cars simultaneously! The Judería (old Jewish Quarter) is a delightful area of tiny streets and white houses. Brilliantly coloured flowers adorn small squares and patios can be seen through doorways.

✉ 187km north of Málaga 🚌 Estación de Autobuses, Plaza de las Tres Culturas ☎ 957 40 40 40 🚆 Estación de RENFE, Avenida de América ☎ 957 40 02 02 ? Easter ceremonies; Flamenco (5–18 May); International Festival of Music, Theatre and Dance (Aug); National Festival of Folklore (Sep) ℹ Tourist information: Calle Torrijos 10 ☎ 957 47 12 35; **www.**turiscordoba.es

DISCOVER CÓRDOBA

ALCÁZAR DE LOS REYES CRISTIANOS

This Mudéjar-style palace was begun by King Alfonso XI in the early 14th century. Outstanding Roman mosaics, the old Moorish courtyard and baths still remain. This was once the residence of the Catholic Kings, and a one-time Moorish prison.

LA MEZQUITA (➤ 26–28)

MUSEO ARQUEOLÓGICO PROVINCIAL

Housed in the attractive 16th-century Palacio de los Páez, the museum has a fine collection of objects, ranging from prehistoric to Roman and Moorish times.

✉ Plaza Jerónimo Páez 7 ☎ 957 47 40 11 🕘 Wed–Sat 9–8:30, Tue 2:30–8:30, Sun 9–2:30 🖐 Cheap (EU citizens free)

Following page: *Cordoba's Alcazar de los Reyes Cristianos*

MUSEO DE BELLAS ARTES

This fine arts museum contains paintings and sculptures by some of Spain's great masters including Goya, Luis Maroles and Alonso.

✉ Plaza de Potro, 1 ☎ 957 47 33 45 ⌚ Wed–Sat 9–8:30, Tue 2:30–8:30 Sun 9–2:30 ✋ Inexpensive

MUSEO MUNICIPAL TAURINO

The Municipal Bullfighting Museum, housed in an elegant 16th-century mansion, has an unusual and fascinating display of items and memorabilia relating to some of Córdoba's most famous bullfighters, including the legendary Manolete.

✉ Plaza Maimónides 5 ☎ 957 20 10 56 ⌚ Oct–Apr, Tue–Sat 10–2, 4:30–6:30; May–Sep 10–2, 6–8; Sun 9:30–2:30 ✋ Inexpensive (free Fri)

PALACIO DE VIANA

The Viana Palace warrants a visit, if only to see the beautiful patios and gardens of this fine 15th-century building. There are collections of paintings, porcelain, furniture and tapestries worth seeing. Note the spendid Mudéjar ceiling above the stairway to the first floor. Visitors are given a one-hour guided tour.

Rejas de Don Gome 2 957 48 01 34 Oct–May, Mon–Fri 10–1, 4–6, Sat 10–1; mid-Jun to Sep 9–2. Closed 1–15 Jun, Sun, public hol Inexpensive Few

TORRE DE LA CALAHORRA

Housed in the 14th-century Moorish fortress across the river, the Museo Histórico (Córdoba City Museum) makes clever use of multivision presentations to trace the history of Córdoba at the height of its golden era.

Puente Romano 957 29 39 29 Daily 10–6 Inexpensive

ESTEPONA

Some 36km west of Marbella is Estepona, another of the Costa del Sol's popular fast developing resorts. It offers the attractions of a long beach, pleasant seafront promenade, a marina and at least three golf courses. It is also a good centre for sailing and windsurfing.

This former fishing village retains a large fleet protected by a harbour which also has moorings for some 400 yachts and pleasure craft. An enjoyable pastime is to take a wander down to the port early in the morning and watch the fresh catch being sold at the fish market.

The old town dates back to Roman and Moorish times. Its focal point is the charming little square of the Plaza de las Flores, entered by four archways of trees. Amid trim orange trees and tropical plants, this is a good place in which to linger over a drink. The surrounding area offers a pleasant stroll through tiny streets lined with picturesque houses. Take a look at the church on Plaza de la Roloj and go down the steps to the Mercado Municipal, a covered market for fruit, vegetables and fresh fish. Above the little town are old castle ruins.

✉ 82km west of Málaga ⇔ Puerto Duquesa (13km west) (➤ 112–13) ? Fiesta de San Isidro (15 May); local festival (early Jul); Fiesta de Virgen del Carmen (16 Jul) i Tourist information: Avenida San Lorenzo 1 ☎ 952 80 09 13/20 02; **www.estepona.es**

FRIGILIANA

It is well worth taking a short drive of some 6km up into the hills from Nerja to visit Frigiliana. This pretty little village, which has won awards for its looks, spreads its dazzlingly whitewashed houses out over the hills in two sections. The older part is a mass of narrow, cobbled streets winding their way up the hillside with wonderful views over fertile orchards and the coast. Here and there you may come across a donkey patiently carrying its load. Streets and balconies are decked out with colourful flowers. The town continues to attract a growing number of visitors, with more shops and restaurants springing up all over.

One of the last battles between the Christians and the Moors was fought in the area in the 16th century, resulting in victory for the Christians. The tale of this exciting event is related by way of a series of ceramic tiles on the walls of the houses.

✉ 56km east of Málaga 🚌 Local ♿ Few ⇔ Nerja (➤ 127)
? Día de la Cruz (3 May); Fería de San Antonio (13 Jun)
ℹ Tourist information: Plaza del Ingenio, s/n ☎ 952 53 31 26

FUENTE VAQUEROS

Fuente Vaqueros is home to the **Casa Museo García Lorca**. The museum was the former home of the poet and playwright Federico García Lorca, who was born in Fuente Vaqueros in 1898. Lorca, who spent much time in nearby Granada, became known for the sensitivity of his poetry and the powerful drama of his plays, such as *Yerma*, *Blood Wedding* and *The House of Bernarda Alba*, which continue to be widely produced in theatres throughout the world. He was assassinated near Viznar during the Spanish Civil War.

17km west of Granada

Casa Museo Federico García Lorca

Calle poeta García Lorca, 4 958 51 64 53 Tue–Sun 10–1, 4–8 (winter 4–6). Tours hourly Inexpensive

CAFETERIA
La Plaza
Banco Zaragozano
Coca-Cola

FUENGIROLA

Some 9km west of Benalmádena Costa is the prominent resort of Fuengirola. It has changed unrecognisably from its earlier days as a peaceful little fishing village. Now the scene is one of solid high-rise apartment blocks and buildings. The old part of the town, however, presents another side of Fuengirola. A lively meeting place is the Plaza de la Constitución, which is dominated by Fuengirola's main church. The old fishermen's district of Santa Fé has plenty of character and high above the town is the old Moorish Castle, Castillo de Sohail.

The castle, which is thought to have originated with the Romans, was rebuilt by the Moors only to be destroyed in the 15th century during the Christian reconquest of the region. The present structure dates from 1730 when it was again reinforced as protection against the British. Castilo de Sohail is now being converted into a cultural centre. A walk up here is recommended for excellent views of the coast.

Fuengirola is much favoured by northern Europeans who come here for extended stays to escape their native winters. There are many English-run bars and souvenir shops to be found here and in neighbouring Los Boliches. The summer season is always lively; the long sweep of beach especially appeals to families. Fuengirola has several other attractions for children, such as the small zoo, an Aquapark at nearby Mijas Costa and the ever-popular Tivoli World up the road.

All kinds of watersports can be enjoyed here too, including sailing, waterskiing and windsurfing. The resort has an attractive yacht club and marina, along with an extended promenade, the Paseo Marítimo, which links Fuengirola, Los Boliches and Carvajal. The former fishing village of Los Boliches has become an extension of Fuengirola, its beach lined with apartment blocks, bars and restaurants. Farther east is the small resort of Carvajal, which has so far retained a more Spanish flavour.

✉ 29km west of Málaga 🚌 Corner Avenida Ramón y Cajal and Calle Alfonso XIII 🚆 RENFE station at Avenida Jesús Santos Rein (half hourly service to Málaga) ♿ Good ⇔ Mijas (➤ 30–31), Parque Aquático (➤ 225) ? Fiesta de la Virgen del Carmen (16 Jul) in Los Boliches; Romería (late Sep) from Fuengirola; Fería del Rosario (7 Oct) ℹ Tourist Information: Paseo Jesús Santos Rein 6 ☎ 952 46 74 57; www.fuengirola.org

GAUCÍN

Situated about 40 minutes drive from the coast between Casares and Ronda, Gaucín is yet another of those enchanting little white towns you will come across travelling around the Andalucían countryside. As you approach you will be confronted by a cluster of whitewashed houses, topped by red roofs, spread out beneath cracked rocks.

The old Moorish fortress, Castillo de Aguila (Eagle's Castle), now partly restored, stands high above the village, forming a silhouette against the backdrop of mountains. From this vantage point there are magnificent views across the valley of the Guadiaro river, reaching out to the coastline as far as the Rock of Gibraltar.

The village is delightful and abounds with colourful flowers and plants. Its narrow streets and one-way system are not conducive to driving, however, and the place is best explored on foot. The daily fish market is always a lively event.

Gaucín makes a good base from which to explore the hinterland, which is dotted about with attractive towns and villages such as Ronda, Grazalema, Casares, Ubrique and Jimena de la Frontera.

✉ 120km west of Málaga 🍴 Several restaurants 🚌 Local bus services ⇔ Casares (➤ 21) ? Romería San Juan (23 Jun); Fería Virgen de las Nieves (second week Aug); Fiesta de Santo Niño (8, 9 and 10 Sep) ℹ Tourist information: Calle Fuente 91, Casares ☎ 952 89 41 26

drive

This drive takes you along the coast through the Sotogrande development to the tiny British colony of Gibraltar.

From Estepona take the N340 coastal road southwest in the direction of Algeciras.

The road follows the coast fairly closely for a while, passing through a string of *urbanizaciones* (developments). Some 10 minutes on you may wish to turn off to Duquesa Marina (follow the signs), another of the Costa's yacht-filled harbours.

Continue on N340.

Soon enter the province of Cádiz and the community of Manilva. Continue through Sotogrande. Shortly after is a turning to Puerto Sotogrande, another marina.

Continue on the N340.

This last section of the coastal road has been widened to dual carriageway. Ticket offices advertising ferry trips to Tangier and Centa signal the approach to the ferry ports.

Soon after, look for the turn-off to La Linea and follow the signs to La Linea–Gibraltar, 7km. Drive to La Linea and continue to the border with Gibraltar.

You are strongly advised to park in La Linea where there are ticket machines (free parking on Sunday). Cross into Gibraltar on foot (passport required). Guides will take you on a 60- to 90-minute a drive through town and up to St Michael's Cave and the dramatic rock formations. The drive continues steeply up through hairpin bends to see the famous apes, and the views of the Mediterranean, Atlantic and south to Africa.

Return to La Linea and take the N240 back to Estepona.

Distance 105km **Time** About 6 hours, allowing time to visit Gibraltar **Start/end point** Estepona **Lunch** Da Paolo (€€) ✉ The Tower, Admiral's Walk, Gibraltar ☎ 9567 76 799

GRANADA

Granada is the capital of its province, the see of an archbishop and a university town. In addition to La Alhambra, with which Granada is so closely associated, the city has much else to commend it: its beautiful setting, built on three hills backed by the snowy peaks of the Sierra Nevada, its historic links with the past and significant religious festivals. A visit to Granada could be made from the coast within a day. However, more time is recommended to explore one of Spain's crowning glories, the last kingdom of the Moors.

Known as Iliberis during the Iberian culture, Granada was taken by the Romans and the Visigoths before its conquest by the Moors in 711. The 11th century saw the decline of the Caliphate of Córdoba and the beginning of the Kingdom of Granada. From the 13th century, until its downfall at the end of the 15th century, Granada flourished as a prosperous cultural centre with the construction of magnificent buildings such as

Fountains at the summer palace of El Generalife

La Alhambra (➤ 18–20). In 1492 Granada was taken by the Catholic Monarchs. This marked the end of Moorish rule and Spain's history was changed. Granada continued to prosper during the Renaissance but a decline set in after the repression of a Moorish uprising in the 16th century.

The priority for most visitors is La Alhambra. Magical as this Moorish palace is, it is surrounded by equally fascinating places including the summer palace of El Generalife, with its shady avenues, water gardens and gazebos. On the slopes of the hill facing La Alhambra is the old Moorish quarter of Albaicín, a labyrinth of steep, narrow streets and small squares which has changed little with time. To the east rises the hill of Sacramonte, once the home of cave-dwelling gypsies.

✉ 129km northeast of Málaga 🚌 Estación de Autobuses, Carretera de Jaén s/n ☎ 958 18 54 80/98 🚆 Estación de FFCC, Avenida de Andalucía s/n ☎ 958 20 40 00 ❓ Día de la Toma (1, 2 Jan); Semana Santa (Easter); Corpus Christi, International Music and Dance Festival (end Jun, early Jul); Romería (29 Sep); International Jazz Festival (Nov) ℹ Tourist information: Corral del Carbón, Plaza de Mariana Pineda, 10 Bajo ☎ 958 24 71 28; **www.**turismodegranada.es

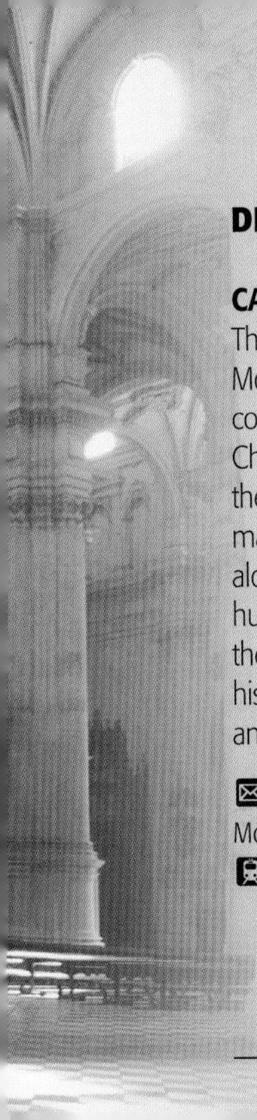

DISCOVER GRANADA

CAPILLA REAL

The Royal Chapel, sanctioned by the Catholic Monarchs for their burial, was begun in 1506 and completed under the reign of Hapsburg Emperor Charles V in 1521. It has a richly adorned interior. In the chancel, closed by a screen, are the mausoleums of King Ferdinand and Queen Isabella, along with their daughter Juana la Loca and her husband Philip the Fair. A museum reached through the north arm of the transept displays items of historical interest and a fine collection of paintings and sculpture.

Oficios 3 (Cathedral) 958 22 78 48 Apr–Oct Mon–Sat 10:30–1, 4–7, Sun 11–1, 4–7 Inexpensive RENFE station Granada

CASA MANUEL DE FALLA

Manuel de Falla (1876–1946) was born in Cadiz and taught by Pedrell, the founder of Spain's modern national school of composition. He spent several years in Paris, but drew on his own native musical traditions in works such as the popular ballet music *The Three-Cornered Hat*. The composer lived in this house for a number of years. Items on display relate to his life.

✉ Antequerela Alta 11 ☎ 958 22 21 89 🕐 Oct–Mar Tue–Fri 10–1, 4–7, Sat and Sun 10–1 ✋ Inexpensive

CATEDRAL

The cathedral was begun in 1528 on the orders of the Catholic Monarchs. Construction was under the great master Diego de Siloé, and continued after his death in 1528. It features a magnificent Capilla Real (Royal Chapel) and has a notable rotunda, with some fine paintings by Alonso Cano, a native of Granada.

✉ Gran Vía 5 ☎ 958 22 29 59 🕐 Mon–Sat 10:30–1:30, 4–7, Sun 4–7 ✋ Inexpensive

MONASTERIO DE LA CARTUJA

This former Carthusian Monastery, which dates back to the 16th century, has a worthwhile collection of paintings and sculpture.

✉ Paseo de la Cartuja, s/n ☎ 958 16 19 32 🕐 Mon–Sat 10–1, 4–6:30 ✋ Inexpensive (free Sun)

MUSEO ARQUEOLÓGICO

The museum is housed in the Casa Castril, an elegant Renaissance palace, noted for its delicately carved plateresque doorway. It has a fine collection of ceramics from Roman and Moorish times, in addition to some superb Egyptian vases unearthed in the region.

✉ Carrera del Darro 41 ☎ 958 22 56 40 🕐 Wed–Sat 9–6, Tue 2:30–6, Sun 9–2:30 ✋ Inexpensive (EU citizens free)

MARBELLA

Marbella's development can be traced back to the 1940s, when Spanish aristocrat Ricardo Soriano founded El Rodeo restaurant and inn. His nephew, Prince Alfonso Hohenlohe of Liechtenstein, went on to develop a small beach property into the Marbella Club chalet complex for his friends among the international set. This continued to attract celebrities to the area and led to the construction of a string of luxurious hotels which were built along the coast on either side of Marbella town, offering beautiful gardens, pools and sports facilities.

After the halcyon days of the 1970s and early '80s, there was an economic slump. Marbella went into a decline and waned popularity. Then in the early 1990s, ambitious programmes were put forward to give the resort a much needed facelift. The remodelling of the Paseo Marítimo, the planting of palms and beautifying of the beaches, along with the construction of underground car parks and pledges to clean the place up in general, did much to restore Marbella's image and prestige. Marbella continues to prosper and grow. Urban developments spread out in all directions, while more projects are underway to propagate the image of the 'New Marbella'.

There are several Marbellas – the town itself, now a busy commercial centre, the beachfront and marina, and its picturesque old quarter, the Casco Antiguo (Old Town) (➤ 29). In the centre of Marbella town there are plush apartments overlooking the sea. From the Casco Antiguo a short walk will take you to the Parque de la Alameda (Alameda Park). The pleasant little park features exotic plants, trees and fountains, with attractively tiled benches adding to the scene. Stroll down to the beachfront through the Avenida del Mar, a broad pedestrianised avenue adorned with flowers and trees and a series of lively Salvador Dalí sculptures.

The Paseo Marítimo, which stretches far on either side of town, offers an enjoyable seafront stroll, with bars and restaurants lining the route. Many improvements have been made to the long stretch of beach, shaded at regular intervals by palm trees. Have a wander around the Puerto Deportivo (yacht harbour), where you can linger over a drink or a meal.

Two museums (in and around the Old Town) are worth a visit; the Museo Bonsai, for its Japanese-style minature trees and the Museo del Grabado Español Contemporáneo (Museum of Spanish Contemporary Prints) for its exhibitions which include works by prominent Spanish artists.

The municipality of Marbella covers a 28km stretch of coastline, which stretches from the marina and the residential area of Cabo Pino, east of the town, to Guadalmina out to the west. The section from Marbella to Guadalmina has come to be known as the Golden Mile, so named for the concentration of luxurious hotels, restaurants and golf courses to be found here. Expensive villas with pools, set amidst gardens of lush, tropical vegetation complete the picture.

References to the 'exclusive resort of Marbella' can be misleading as, more often than not, the term applies not to the town, but to the hotels strung out on either side of the town, including the Guadalmina development and the Puerto Banús marina. This area is, in effect, the 'playground' of the jet set.

Puerto Banús (➤ 34–37) is officially part of San Pedro de Alcántara (➤ 138–39, located 3km away) and is usually listed under Nueva Andalucía. However, it is within the community of Marbella and tends to be included in references to the town. It continues to be a place of pure enjoyment and a magnet for yachties. The marina has berths for over 900 and attracts craft of all sizes. There are also watersports facilities.

Marbella continues to attract celebrities and stars. The partying goes on but has become less visible as more of the social scene takes place privately. This does not deter many visitors, however, who may well catch sight of some familiar faces.

56km west of Málaga Bus station, Avenida del Trapiche, s/n 952 76 44 00. Avenida Ricardo Soriano for local services Carnival (pre-Lent), Feria de la Virgen del Carmen (16 Jul), Feria de San Bernabé Patrón (Jun), Feria de San Pedro (Oct) Glorieta de la Fontanilla, Paseo Marítimo 952 77 14 42. Plaza de los Naranjos 952 82 35 50

MIJAS (➤ 30–31)

NERJA

Nerja lies in a fertile valley of fruit orchards, known mainly for the production of peaches and pomegranates. Its attractive setting amidst cliffs overlooking the rocky coves below have earned its reputation as the jewel of the eastern Costa del Sol. Its name is derived from the old Moorish word *naricha*, meaning 'rich in water'. The town started life as a Moorish farming estate during the 10th century, a centre of the silk and sugar industries for the area. All reminders of its Moorish past and much of the town were destroyed in the devastating earthquake of 1884.

Nerja stands out as the most appealing of the resorts east of Málaga. It retains the charm of its old town with its narrow streets, many pedestrianised, and lined with whitewashed houses that are adorned with flowers, and crammed with restaurants. These streets lead down to Nerja's best-known feature and focal point, the Bálcon de Europa. This curved promontory, lined with palm trees overlooking the bay is a favoured spot for keen photographers. A series of steps will take you down to the Paseo de los Caribineros and a walkway onto the popular Plays de Burriana.

Although Nerja has grown into an internationally popular resort over the years, it has so far managed to escape the sort of development found along much of its neighbouring western coastline. Most noticeably Nerja has managed to retain its small-town atmosphere. Now linked to Málaga by the Autovía del Mediterraneo, expansion is inevitably on its way, with some new developments to be seen along the seafront.

Some 4km east of Nerja lies the little village of Maro. Perched on a clifftop above a small cove, the village offers good views of the coastline. Of interest is the attractive little church of Nuestra Señora de las Maravillas de Maro, and the four-tiered aqueduct.

52km east of Málaga Bus connections Maro (4km east) Carnival (pre-Lent); Semana Santa (Easter); Cruces de Mayo (3 May); Fiesta de la Virgen del Carmen (16 Jul); Feriá de Nerja (13 Oct) Tourist information: Puerta del Mar 4 952 52 15 31

RINCÓN DE LA VICTORIA

Lying some 12km east of Málaga, Rincón de la Victoria is a fast-developing resort. It offers a pleasant new seafront promenade, some modest accommodation, an 18-hole golf course, riding, tennis and boats for hire. The resort has a reputation for good fish restaurants, a speciality being a small sardine-type fish known as *victorianos* and *coquinas* (clams). The Wednesday market is always a great event.

✉ 12km east of Málaga ? Fiesta de la Virgen del la Candelaria (1–3 Feb); Fiesta de la Virgen del Carmen (16 Jul); Fiesta de Verano (22–25 Aug) ℹ Granada 2 B ☎ 952 40 77 68

The shrine of the Virgin del Carmen, above Rincón de la Victoria

RONDA

Ronda is renowned for its spectacular setting. The views of the ravine and the surrounding landscapes, its historical background and legends of bandits, all add to a certain mystique, which continues to attract visitors. A mighty split in the El Tajo Gorge, spanned by the Puente Nuevo (➤ 32–33), divides the town into Old Ronda (La Ciudad) and the newer part, known as El Mercadillo.

Most monuments of note are in the old town, which retains Moorish influences. These include the imposing church of Santa Maria la Mayor, the Minaret of San Sebastian, the Palacio de Mondragón and the Casa del Gigante, the Palacio del Marqués de Salvatierra and the gardens of the Casa del Rey Moro. The Museo Lara (Science and History) and Museo del Bandolero (History and Legends of local bandits) are also worth a visit. The café-lined Plaza del Socorro is the focal point of the newer part of town, Ronda's main shopping centre, with more magnificent views to be seen from the attractive gardens of the Alameda del Tajo, near by.

Ronda has long-standing associations with bullfighting. The bullring, near the Puente Nuevo, was built in 1785 and is the

oldest in Spain. It was here that the rules of modern bullfighting were laid down by Francisco Romero, whose grandson Pedro Romero went on to become one of Spain's most famous matadors. The bullring, now owned by Antonio Ordoñez, another of the greats, is used only for special fiestas. The bullfighting museum behind the ring contains glittering costumes, gear and a wealth of photographs relating to the world of bullfighting.

Ronda is a city with a romantic past. Two famous Americans, writer Ernest Hemingway and actor Orson Welles, were keen followers of the bullfight. Both spent much time here and each of them formed a close friendship with Ordoñez. By his request, Orson Welles' ashes are scattered over the bulfighter's nearby ranch.

Some 20km southwest of Ronda is the **Cueva de la Pileta** (Pileta Cave), which has significant prehistoric rock paintings of animals, outlined in black and red, believed to date back to over 25,000 years ago. The illustrated figures include bison, deer, horses and a large fish.

118km northwest of Málaga Buses from Algeciras, Málaga (via Bobadilla) Pedro Romero Festival (► 116) Plaza de España 1 952 87 12 72

Cueva de la Pileta

20km southwest of Ronda 952 16 73 43 Daily 10–1, 4–6; tours last about one hour Inexpensive

walk

This walk starts in the Plaza de España and takes you across the bridge to explore the old town.

From the Plaza de España walk towards the Puente Nuevo (New Bridge).

Walk around the Parador, on your right, for views of the gorge.

Return and cross over the bridge.

Look down into the ravine. Turn right down Calle Tenorio to a network of narrow streets to the Plaza del Campillo.

Keep walking and at the far end look for steps leading down the hill.

A short walk down reveals Ronda's houses on the clifftop.

Back up again take the street ahead to Plaza Mondragón.

On the right is the Moorish Palacio de Mondragón.

Continue to Plaza de la Duquesa de Parcént. Turn left to the Colegiata de Santa María la Mayor. Take the short slope down to Calle Armiñian and turn left. Note the Minaret of San Sebastian before crossing over to turn sharp right.

There are fine carvings on the façade of the Palacio del Marqués de Salvatierra (closed to the public).

Climb up Calle Santo Domingo to the Casa del Rey Moro, where you can take a long winding staircase down to the river and back up again to the gardens. Rejoin Calle Armiñán and cross over the bridge to the Plaza de España.

Distance 4km **Time** 2–3 hours **Start/end point** Plaza de España
Lunch Pedro Romero (€€) ✉ Virgen de la Paz 18, Ronda
☎ 952 87 11 10

SALOBREÑA

Some 13km east of Almuñecar is the attractive little town of Salobreña, now within the stretch of coast known as the Costa Tropical. It lies a short distance from the sea among fruit orchards and sugarcane plantations.

Salobreña features a cluster of whitewashed houses sprawling up the hill, dominated by the old Moorish *alcázar* known as El Capricho. The castle has been well restored and offers magnificent

views of the coast, surrounding countryside and the beautiful peaks of the Sierra Nevada. Also worth a visit is the 16th-century church of Nuestra Señora del Rosario, which was built on the site of an old mosque.

Much of Salobreña's charm lies in the fact that it remains relatively unspoilt, with few hotels and restaurants. It provides a good gateway to Granada, however, and can receive quite an influx of visitors, especially at weekends. From here it is only 4km farther along the coast to Motril, principally known as a commercial centre for sugarcane and chemicals. Take a look at the Sanctuary of Our Lady of the Head, which stands atop the hill. Enthusiasts enjoy the golf course, located between the two.

☒ 93 km east of Málaga ▣ Bus connections ⇔ Almuñecar (13km west, ➤ 80–81) ? Semana Santa (Easter): Fiesta de San Juan y San Pedro (end Jul); Fiesta de Nuestra Señora del Rosario (early Oct) ℹ Tourist information: Plaza de Goya s/n ☎ 958 61 03 14

The castle at Salobrena

SAN PEDRO DE ALCÁNTARA

San Pedro Alcántara has undergone a facelift in recent years with pleasing results. A development programme incorporating a new promenade and beach improvements, stretching from Puerto Banús to Guadalmina, has given it a boost as an increasingly popular resort.

On the northern side of the coastal road is the small town itself, which has a neat, pleasant appearance. The Calle Marqués del Duero, shaded by orange trees and palms, and lined with shops and cafés, leads up the hill to the small square of Plaza de la Iglesia. Adjacent to the town hall is San Pedro's parish church. Its white façade framed by two palm trees makes an attractive picture.

San Pedro is the first centre in Spain to have introduced the sport of cable skiing, which involves the water skier being towed by cable for long distances.

Three archaeological sites in the vicinity are worth exploring: the 6th-century Visigoth Basílica de Vega del Mar, the Villa Romana de Río Verde, remnants of a Roman villa from the 1st century, and Las Bovedas where the remains of old Roman thermal baths can be seen.

70km west of Málaga Tourist information: Avenida Marques del Duero, 69 952 78 52 52

SAN ROQUE/SOTOGRANDE

This is *the* place for big-time golfers. Among the four golf courses, the Valderrama Robert Trent Jones Course played host to the 1997 Ryder Cup. Polo is also played here during the summer and the Sotogrande Marina is another attraction. The little town is an attractive centre in itself with narrow streets and plenty of flowers and plants. The lively cafés and restaurants of the Campamento area appeal to a younger crowd.

100km west of Málaga Bus connections San Roque Annual Fair (early Sep); Sotogrande golf tournaments, polo matches (Jul, Aug, Sep) Avda 20 Abril s/n, La Línea 956 76 99 50

drive

This drive takes you into the rugged landscape of the Serranía de Ronda and through several of the region's most attractive mountain towns.

From the east side of San Pedro de Alcántara, take the turning to Ronda (➤ 130–33).

The A376, (Ruta de la Serranía de Ronda) is fairly wide and has a good surface as it twists its way up into the mountains. The route takes you through pine forests, rocks and white cliffs, until Ronda comes into view, about an hour later (50km). Visit Ronda and have some lunch at the restaurant which offers a dramatic view of the steep cliff on which the town is built.

Return through the old town and take the A369, in the direction of Algeciras, to Gaucín (➤ 110–11).

This section passes through barren hills and rocks and wide open vistas and includes a bad stretch of road. Take a look at the delightful white hillside town of Gaucín.

Join the A377, direction Manilva-Algeciras. Some 16km on take a sharp left turn to the town of Casares (➤ 21).

This road leads to a stunning view of this Andalucían town. Continue towards Casares and fork left uphill for an even more spectacular sight of the town, crowned by the old fortress.

Follow the signs to Estepona and take the old road, which winds its way down through fertile country to the coast. You should reach Estepona some 25 minutes later (➤ 102). Rejoin N340 and head east back to San Pedro.

Distance 145km **Time** About 8 hours **Start/end point** San Pedro de Alcántara **Lunch** Hotel-Restaurante Don Miguel, Ronda (€€)
✉ Villanueva 4 y 8, Ronda ☎ 952 87 10 90

SEVILLA

Sevilla is the capital of Andalucía and Spain's fourth largest city. It is dominated by La Giralda and the great cathedral that this minaret tower adjoins (➤ 24–25). Various cultures have left their mark here, from the Romans to the Moors and the Christians. An early carving on the Jerez Gate alludes to the legendary origins of the city: 'Hercules built me, Caesar surrounded me with walls and towers, the King Saint took me.'

Sevilla is believed to have been founded by the Iberians. Subsequent occupiers included the Greeks, Phoenicians and the Carthaginians (who named it Hispalis). Around 205BC the town was taken over by the Romans and it continued to flourish under Julius Caesar. During the 5th century AD it

became the capital of the Visigoths. It was captured in 712 by the Moors, whose long occupation has left magnificent traces of their artistic merits.

In 1248 Sevilla was reconquered by Ferdinand III of Castille. But it was the discovery of America which brought fame and prosperity to Sevilla, when Christopher Columbus returned here from his first voyage in 1493. In the 16th and 17th centuries the port became the most important in Spain. During this period, often described as Spain's Golden Age, the Sevilla school of painters brought great prestige to the city.

Sevilla is a city to explore on foot, the cathedral is a good point from which to start. The medieval quarter of the Barrio Santa Cruz, near by, is a delightful maze of narrow streets and whitewashed houses adorned with wrought-iron balconies, decked with flowers.

A stroll around town reveals mansions, squares and lovely parks, such as the Parque de Maria Luisa, the Murillo gardens and those of the Reales Alcazares. The large Plaza de España contains a tiny canal, decorated bridges and fountains. An imposing crescent is adorned with ceramic tiles depicting Spain's provincial capitals.

Over the bridge is the Triana area, home of the gypsy population. Alternative ways of getting around are by 'SevillaTour' buses or with style in a horse-drawn carriage.

Well known as the setting for *Carmen* and other operas, Sevilla has long had a romantic image. In the spring, when the scent of orange blossom gives Sevilla a special atmosphere, the unique celebrations of Semana Santa (Holy Week) and the exuberant Fería de Sevilla take place (➤ 228–29).

The Isla Mágica theme park, on the Isla de la Cartuja, is dedicated to the Century of the Discoveries.

✉ 219km northwest of Málaga 🚌 Bus stations: Prado de San Sebastían ☎ 954 41 71 11 & Plaza de Armas ☎ 954 90 77 37 🚆 Estación de FFCC Santa Justa, Avenida Kansas City s/n ☎ 954 54 02 02 ❓ Semana Santa (Easter), Fería de Sevilla (2 weeks after Easter), Corpus Christi, Fiesta de la Virgen de los Reyes (15 Aug) ℹ Avenida de la Constitucíon 21 B ☎ 954 22 14 04

DISCOVER SEVILLA

CASA DE PILATOS

This 16th-century private mansion is one of Sevilla's jewels. Combining Mudéjar, Gothic and Renaissance styles, its patios, archways and salons are adorned with delicate carving, tilework and wooden coffered ceilings. A grand staircase leads to the upper floors, which contain a collection of art. The adjoining gardens may also be visited.

✉ Plaza Pilatos 1 ☎ 954 22 52 98 ⏲ Daily 9–6 🚌 C1, C2, C3, C4
♿ Good 💰 Inexpensive (free Tue pm)

MUSEO ARQUEOLÓGICO

Housed in the Renaissance palace built for the 1929 Ibero-America Exhibition, the Archeological Museum has a fine collection of objects from prehistory and the Moorish culture. Outstanding among its exhibits is the Carombolo Treasure; from the 7th century this includes gold jewellery from the Tartessos civilisation.

✉ Plaza de América ☎ 954 23 24 01 ⏲ Wed–Sat 9–8, Tue 3–8, Sun, pub hol 9–2 Inexpensive (EU citizens free)

MUSEO DE BELLAS ARTES

Housed in the former Convento de la Merced, the museum contains a collection of fine art with paintings and sculpture, ceramics and weapons. Room V contains works of art by some of the great Spanish masters, including Zurbarán and Murillo.

Plaza Museo 9 954 22 07 90 Wed–Sat 9–8, Tue 3–8, Sun, pub hol 9–2 Inexpensive (EU citizens free)

REALES ALCÁZARES

Former Moorish palaces, largely rebuilt for Christian kings after the reconquest of Sevilla: the centrepiece, Palacio Mudéjar del Rey Don Pedro, built by Pedro I in the 14th century, is a superb example of Mudéjar art. Salons, archways and columns are richly decorated with exquisite carvings, ceramics and wooden ceilings. Note the dome ceiling of the Salón de Embajadores (Hall of Ambassadors).

Plaza del Triunfo 954 50 23 23 Tue–Sat 9:30–7, Sun 9:30–5 Moderate C1, C2, C3, C4 Go early if possible. Restrictions on numbers allowed in during busy periods can result in queues

TARIFA

To stand on the Punta de Tarifa is to be at the southernmost point of Europe, with the coast of the African continent only 14km away. Located on the fringe of the Costa del Sol, Tarifa has a totally different flavour about it which in itself makes a visit worthwhile.

The town has played an important role in the history of the Iberian peninsula. It was named after Tarif Ibn Malik, the Moorish leader who in 710 arrived here from north Africa with a small band of men and took possession of the area. This led to the larger invasion which took place the following year and the subsequent Moorish conquest of most of present-day Spain. Tarifa was taken by the Christians in 1292 but the siege was maintained for the next couple of years.

Entrance to the town, which is encircled by walls, is through a Moorish gate. With its dazzling white houses and maze of narrow, winding streets, Tarifa retains a distinctive Moorish look. The port offers a good view of the old Moorish castle above the town, which is in the hands of the Spanish Navy and not open to the public.

Tarifa is blessed by a long expanse of sandy beach backed by pine trees. This marks the meeting point of the Mediterranean and the Atlantic and the strong winds which sweep across the sand create excellent conditions for windsurfing in the bay. The place has now become a top centre for the sport, with kitesurfing fast gaining in popularity.

☒ 21km west of Algeciras 🚌 Bus connections with Algeciras ⇔ Roman ruins at Baelo Claudia at Bolonia (14km northwest on N340, 9km off main road to Bolonia Cove) ? Día de los Reyes (6 Jan); Carnival (pre-Lent); Romería del Consejo (15 May); Fiesta de San Juan (24 Jun); Fiesta de la Virgen del Carmen (16 Jul); National Folk Music Festival (early Aug); Fiesta de Nuestra Señora de la Luz (early Sep) ℹ Paseo de la Alameda ☎ 956 68 09 93; **www**.tarifaweb.com

TORRE DEL MAR

Located in the eastern Costa de Sol, Torre del Mar is the beach resort of Vélez-Málaga, capital of the Axarquía region.

There are unsubstantiated claims that Torre del Mar once formed part of an ancient Greek settlement known as Mainake which is believed to have been destroyed by the Carthaginians, before the arrival of the Romans. These days the town consists primarily of a long beach lined with high-rise apartment blocks catering mainly for summer visitors.

One of the resort's most pleasant features is the extended esplanade which follows the coast, to reach the marina of Caleta de Vélez. With over 200 berths, it presents an attractive scene of boats and yachts, offering sailing and a variety of other watersports. Its lively cafés and restaurants also provide a good place in which to idle the time away. Another bonus is the good seafood served here in numerous eateries.

☒ 30km east of Málaga 🚌 Bus connections ⇔ Vélez-Málaga (5km inland, ➤ 161) ? Fiestas at Vélez-Málaga ℹ Tourist information: Avenida de Andalucía 52 ☎ 952 54 11 04

TORREMOLINOS

Torremolinos, 8km west of Málaga airport, heralds the start of the most developed part of the coast. To many, this stretch of coast, lined with high-rise apartment blocks and development as far as Estepona, represents the real Costa del Sol.

Torremolinos began to grow as a holiday resort in the 1950s, when the building of luxury hotels got under way, and it became one of the first places on this coast to cater for mass tourism. Its proximity to Málaga airport is a point in its

favour. At the height of summer the resort has a great appeal for the younger set, with a reputation for its hectic night life. Out of season, however, it takes on a different mantle. The pace slows down and, at weekends in particular, the city appears almost as a suburb of Málaga with Spanish families much in evidence.

There's a definite divide between the town and the beach area below. The main artery of the town is the pedestrianised Calle San Miguel. Lined with a varied assortment of shops and surrounded by numerous bars and restaurants, this mini *ramblas* attracts a constant flow of people. Other popular spots for eating and drinking are the small Andalucian-style development of Pueblo Blanco nearby, and the area of El Calvario, located beyond the top end of San Miguel. A favourite establishment here is the Galloping Major (splendidly translated as El Comandante Galopando), which opened in 1964 as the first English-style pub in Torremolinos.

At the south end of San Miguel the Cuesta del Tajo leads down winding steps crammed with souvenir shops to the El Bajondillo beach.

The beach area shows another side of Torremolinos. With massive hotels, apartment blocks, bars and restaurants, this area is packed during the summer. To the left, the Playa de Bajondillo gives way to the beaches of Playamar and Los Almos. To the right, beyond the Castillo de Santa Clara, lie the beach areas of La Carihuela and Montemar.

The Paseo Marítimo, the seafront promenade, extends east to Playamar and west to La Carihuela, now continuing as far as Benalmádena Costa. The walk to La Carihuela offers pleasant sea views and some dramatic rock formations, before entering the old fishing village of La Carihuela, which is a delightful area of pictureqeue little houses and streets. It has a good reputation for excellent fish and seafood restaurants. In summer, the *chiringuitos* (beach bars) are well worth sampling.

✉ 12km west of Málaga 🚆 Half-hourly to Málaga (25 minutes) and Fuengirola ⇔ Málaga (➤ 40–65) ? Carnival (pre-Lent); Feria de Verdiales (Mar); Easter; Fiesta de la Virgen del Carmen (16 Jul); Día del Turista (early Sep); Feria de San Miguel (late Sep); Romería de San Miguel (Sun, late Sep) ℹ Main office: Ayuntamiento, Plaza Blas Infante 1 ☎ 952 37 95 12. Plaza de la Independencia s/n ☎ 952 37 42 31. Plaza de las Comunidades Autónomas, s/n (Playa de Bajondillo) ☎ 952 37 19 09

drive

This drive offers some striking scenery, taking you first to Antequera and continuing to the bizarre boulders in the El Torcal National Park.

From Torremolinos turn onto the N340 towards Málaga. Passing the airport on your left, continue on the Málaga ring road (Ronda de Málaga) and follow the signs to Antequera (N331).

After the turn off to Finca de la Concepción this excellent highway climbs up through the hills of the Montes de Málaga, scattered with olive groves and tiny white houses. As you approach Antequera strange rock shapes rise from the fertile plains, noticeably the striking form of the so-called Peña de los Enamorados (Lovers' Rock). About an hour after departure you should enter Antequera (➤ 82–83). Allow time to explore this attractive city of churches and convents.

Take the Calle de la Legión, south and just out of town, pause to admire the magnificent views of Antequera on your left, backed by the distinctive form of the Peña de los Enamorados. Take the C3310, following the signs to Torcal.

The road winds through a barren landscape of rocks and boulders for half an hour before reaching a right turn to Parque Natural del Torcal de Antequera. As you drive through the park, the rocks and boulders become increasingly curious, until the whole landscape appears positively lunar-like. The road ends 15 minutes later by a small hut; walking trails start from here.

Rejoin the C3310 and continue south to the coast and return to Torremolinos.

Distance 125 km **Time** About 6 hours **Start/end point** Torremolinos
Lunch Parador de Antequera (€€) ✉ García del Olmo, Antequera
☎ 952 84 02 61

TORROX COSTA

Along the eastern end of the Costa del Sol, situated between Torre del Mar and Nerja, is the resort of Torrox Costa. Torrox consists basically of a long stretch of beach, backed with modern apartment blocks, sympathetically designed with reflections of the Moorish style of architecture. The resort has been developed primarily for visitors in summer, when it bustles. The beach offers watersports, while an extended promenade offers a pleasant stroll along the seafront, with a reasonable choice of restaurants, bars and shops.

Take a look at the church of La Encarnación and the Hermitage of Nuestra Señora de las Nieves, both of which still retain traces of Moorish influences. Scattered along the coast are a few old watchtowers and small fortresses. Some 4km inland lies the old town of Torrox; built up the steep slopes of the hill, its whitewashed houses make an attractive pattern.

✉ 47km east of Málaga 🚌 Bus connections ↔ Competa (18km north, ➤ 92–93), Nerja (6km east, ➤ 127–28) ? Carnival (pre-Lent); La Cruz de Mayo (2 May); Fiesta de San Juan (23–24 Jun); Fiesta de la Virgen de la Nieves (5 Aug); local fair (4–7 Oct) ℹ Centro Internacional, bloque 79 ☎ 952 53 02 25

VÉLEZ-MÁLAGA

The small town of Vélez-Málaga lies 5km inland from Torre del Mar, surrounded by subtropical vegetation. Capital of La Axarquía, it is the centre of an agricultural region known for its production of strawberries and vineyards, which grow the muscatel grapes from which the famous Málaga wines are made. It is also a centre for the processing of olive oil and sugarcane. Ceramics feature among other industries. If you are here on a Thursday, take time to wander around its weekly market, always an enjoyable experience.

The town is crowned by a 13th-century Moorish castle which has been well restored. There are good views of the surrounding countryside from here. The oldest part of the town, Arrabal de San Sebastián, is a picturesque area of narrow streets. Of special note, among the several churches to be found in the town, is the 15th-century church of Santa María la Mayor, which shows the Mudéjar style. This was the first building to be erected by the Christians, following their victory over the Moors here in 1487.

✉ 34km east of Málaga 🚌 Bus connections ⇔ Nerja (➤ 127–28)
ℹ Avenida de Andalucia 119 ☎ 952 54 11 04

Where to eat & drink... Costa del Sol & beyond

ALMUÑÉCAR

BODEGA FRANCISCO (€)

Centrally placed bar/restaurant serving a good selection of tapas at very reasonable prices.

✉ Calle Real 15 ☎ 952 63 01 68 🕒 Lunch and dinner

ANTEQUERA

LA ESPUELA (€€)

Long-established restaurant, within the lower part of the bullring complex. A wide selection of dishes includes local specialities.

✉ Plaza de Toros de Antequera ☎ 952 84 46 62 🕒 Lunch and dinner, closed Mon

ARROYO DE LA MIEL

MESÓN DEL VIRREY (€€€)

In a pleasant old building. Known for good traditional cooking with emphasis on meat dishes. Summer terrace.

✉ Avenida de la Constitución 87 ☎ 952 44 35 99 🕒 Lunch and dinner, closed Wed

VENTORILLO DE LA PERRA (€€€)

Housed in an 18th-century inn. Cosy, attractive patio with plants. Spanish and international dishes.

✉ Avenida de la Constitución 85 ☎ 952 44 19 66 🕒 Lunch and dinner, closed Mon

BENALMÁDENA COSTA

MALAGUETO PUERTO (€€)

Offers good grilled meats and a wide selection of fish dishes. Bream, baked in salt, can be a good bet.

✉ Puerto Marina ☎ 952 44 00 04 🕒 Lunch and dinner

EL MERO (€€)

Top quality restaurant located on first-floor level with views over the marina. Known for its shellfish and barbecued meats.

✉ Dársena de Levante, Puerto Marina ☎ 952 44 07 52 🕒 Lunch and dinner

EL MIRADOR (€€€)

Top class international restaurant offering varied menu and panoramic views of the mountains and the coastline.

✉ Calle Bellavista, Urb Torremuelle (on the Fuengirola–Benalmádena coastal road) ☎ 952 44 33 98 ⌚ Lunch and dinner

BENALMÁDENA PUEBLO

CASA FIDEL (€€)

Rustic atmosphere with large fireplace. International cuisine.

✉ Maestra Ayala 1 ☎ 952 44 91 65 ⌚ Lunch and dinner, closed Tue, Wed lunch, Aug

CÓRDOBA

BANDELERO (€–€€)

Facing the Mezquita with an attractive bar and several dining rooms at the rear. Wide selection of simple dishes and *tapas*.

✉ Calle de Torrijos 6 ☎ 957 47 64 91 ⌚ Lunch and dinner

EL CHURRASCO (€€)

Long-standing restaurant and lively *tapas* bar. Centrally located with attractive patio. Known for grilled meats.

✉ Romero 16 ☎ 957 29 08 17 ⌚ Lunch and dinner, closed Aug

ESTEPONA

BUENAVENTURA (€€€)

Top-quality restaurant offering creative cuisine. Outdoor dining in beautiful courtyard and on the Plaza de la Iglesia, where diners can watch operatic performances in August.

Plaza de la Iglesia 5 952 85 80 69 Lunch and dinner

EL CENACHERO (€€)

Located in the marina. Mediterranean cuisine, specialises in fresh shellfish, *zarzuelas*, fish baked in salt.

Puerto Deportivo 952 80 14 42 Lunch and dinner, closed Tue in winter and 15–30 Nov

MESÓN CORDOBÉS (€€)

Excellent location, with tables out on the attractive Plaza de la Flores. Fish features largely on the menu: the fresh catch of the day is a good bet when its available.

Plaza de la Flores 15 952 80 07 37 Lunch and dinner, closed Sat

LA RADA (€)

Popular for its lively atmosphere and the quality of its fish, seafood and rice dishes.

✉ Avenida de España ☎ 952 79 10 36 🕐 Lunch and dinner, closed Tue

FRIGILIANA

THE GARDEN BAR (€€)

Popular with locals, offering a casual atmosphere and attractive views. Good for barbecued and grilled meats.

✉ In the old part of the town; look for signs ☎ 952 53 31 85 🕐 Lunch and dinner, closed Tue

FUENGIROLA

CRÊPES 'N' BAR (€)

Small hospitable establishment offering more than 50 varieties of French-style crêpes. Eating indoors or al fresco.

✉ Calle Ollerías 15 ☎ 951 31 11 77 🕐 Lunch and dinner, closed Tue

LA LANGOSTA (€€)

Long-established favourite, renowned for lobster dishes.

✉ Calle Francisco Cano 1, Los Boliches ☎ 952 47 50 49 🕐 Dinner only, closed Sun

LE VAGABOND (€€)

French cuisine in this friendly restaurant. Attractive surroundings with a small terrace for outdoor eating in summer. Excellent value.

✉ Calle de la Cruz 14 ☎ 952 46 21 46 🕓 Dinner only, closed Wed

PORTOFINO (€€)

Italian specialities and international dishes in this restaurant on the seafront.

✉ Edificio Perla, Paseo Marítimo 29 ☎ 952 47 06 43
🕓 Lunch and dinner, closed Mon, 1–15 Jul, 1–15 Dec. Dinner only in summer

GRANADA

CHIKITO (€€)

Popular restaurant, once frequented by writers and artists. Bar and restaurant known for its cured ham.

✉ Plaza del Campillo 9 ☎ 958 22 33 64 🕓 Lunch and dinner, closed Wed

ROMERIJO

MIRADOR DE MORAYMA (€€€)

Excellent position with fine views of the Alhambra from its terraces. Country-style decor, lively ambience.

Pianista Gracia Carillo 2 952 22 82 90 Lunch and dinner, closed Sun

SEVILLA (€€)

Old haunt of García Lorca and Manuel de Falla. Attractive dining rooms, open terrace.

Oficios 12 958 22 12 23 Lunch and dinner, closed Sun

MARBELLA

EL BALCÓN DE LA VIRGEN (€)

Delightful small restaurant housed in one of the town's picturesque streets. Andalucian and international cuisine.

Calle Remedios 2 952 77 60 92 Lunch and dinner, closed Sun

CALIFORNIA (€)

Casual ambience, popular with locals. Good-value fish and seafood *tapas*.

Calle Málaga 2, Edif. Sol. No. 2 952 86 67 52 Lunch and dinner, closed Sun

LA HACIENDA (€€€)

Top restaurant with reputation for *haute cuisine*. Good location on a hill with sea views.

✉ Urbanización Las Chapas, N340 (12km east of Marbella) ☎ 952 83 11 16 ⏲ Dinner only in summer; closed Mon, Tue and mid-Nov to mid-Dec

LOS NARANJOS (€€)

Good position right on Plaza de los Naranjos, centre of Marbella's Casco Antiguo. Mediterranean and international cuisine.

✉ Plaza de los Naranjos s/n ☎ 952 77 18 19 ⏲ Lunch and dinner, closed Sun

LA PESQUERA (€)

In the old town. Bar and restaurant serving good seafood.

✉ Plaza de la Victoria s/n ☎ 952 76 51 70 ⏲ Lunch and dinner

LA PESQUERA DEL FARO (€€)

Overlooking the sea, this combines the atmosphere of a beach hotel with good-quality food. Specials include fish baked in salt and seafood dishes. Steps lead down to a terrace right on the beach, adjoining Marbella's marina.

✉ Playa del Faro, Paseo del Marítimo ☎ 952 86 85 20 🕐 Lunch and dinner

MIJAS

MIRLO BLANCO (€€)

Basque and international cuisine. Outdoor terrace overlooking the charming little square of Plaza de la Constitución.

✉ Paseo del Compás ☎ 952 48 57 00 🕐 Lunch and dinner

EL PADTRASTO (€€€)

Spectacularly sited on the clifftop. Terrace with views of Fuengirola and the coast. Top cuisine, offers local specialities and international dishes. Access by lift or a steep flight of stairs.

✉ Paseo del Compás 22 ☎ 952 48 50 00 🕐 Lunch and dinner

LA REJA (€€)

Elevated position offering pleasant views of the town from the terrace. Specialises in grilled meats, fish, seafood and pizzas.

✉ Los Caños 9 ☎ 952 48 69 42 🕐 Lunch and dinner, closed Mon

VALPARAÍSO (€€)

In an attractive villa with a terrace, gardens and a pool, this is ideal for a dinner-dancing evening out.

✉ Carretera de Fuengirola, Km 4 ☎ 952 48 59 96 🕐 Dinner only, closed Sun in winter

NERJA

LA MARINA (€)

Popular with locals and families, this restaurant offers a wide variety of fish dishes and seafood *tapas*.

✉ Plaza de la Marina ☎ 952 52 12 29 🕐 Lunch and dinner

PEPE RICO (€€€)

Top restaurant renowned for the quality of its cuisine. Housed in a mansion, meals are served in an elegant dining room or outside on a flower-filled patio.

✉ Almirante Ferrándiz 28 ☎ 952 52 02 47 🕐 Lunch and dinner, closed Tue, 1–15 Dec, 15 Jan–15 Feb

NUEVA ANDALUCÍA

DIVINA GULA (€€)

International cuisine. Specialities include Argentinian-style

grilled meats, fresh pasta dishes, lamb and fish.
✉ Plaza la Orquídea s/n ☎ 952 81 87 00 🕐 Lunch and dinner

PUERTO BANÚS

AZUL MARINO (€€)

Brasserie-restaurant, good for fish and seafood.
✉ Front Line, Port I ☎ 952 81 10 44 🕐 Lunch and dinner

LA CARACOLA DEL PUERTO (€€)

Restaurant overlooking the quay; known for its varieties of paellas, along with a good selection of *tapas* and other dishes.
✉ Muelle Benabola 5 ☎ 952 81 16 84 🕐 Lunch and dinner, closed Tue

CHRISTIAN BISTRO DU PORT (€€)

One of Puerto Banús's earliest restaurants, ever popular.
✉ In the port ☎ 952 81 10 06 🕐 Lunch and dinner

DON LEONE (€€€)

Italian favourite, open air, overlooking marina.
✉ Muelle Ribera ☎ 952 81 17 16 🕐 Lunch and dinner; closed end-Nov to end-Dec

LA OLA (€€)

Elegant quayside restaurant specialising in paella and rice dishes.

✉ Muelle Ribera ☎ 952 81 14 23 🕒 Lunch and dinner, closed Tue

SALOBREÑA

MESÓN DE LA VILLA (€–€€)

One of the resort's most popular restaurants, with a good reputation for its fish dishes.

✉ Plaza F. Ramírez de Madrid ☎ 958 61 24 14 🕒 Lunch and dinner, closed Wed

SAN PEDRO DE ALCÁNTARA

ALBERT & SIMON (€€€)

Top class restaurant, known for the excellence of its creative French cuisine.

✉ Urb Nueva Alcántara (near Naturae) ☎ 952 78 37 14 🕒 Lunch and dinner, closed Sun

JARDÍN DEL VINO (€€)

On San Pedro's main street, the restaurant offers rustic surroundings, cosy ambience and international cuisine. Terrace

open in summer.
✉ Marqués del Duero 9 ☎ 952 78 42 16 ⌚ Lunch and dinner, closed Wed

VICTOR (€€)
Specialities include rack of lamb, sea bass and good seafood.
✉ Centro Comercial Guadalmina, local 1 ☎ 952 88 34 91 ⌚ Lunch and dinner, closed Sun dinner and Mon

SAN ROQUE

LOS REMOS (€€€)
High class restaurant in a neoclassical villa with attractive gardens. Known for fish and seafood dishes.
✉ Villa Victoria S, Campamento ☎ 956 69 84 12 ⌚ Lunch and dinner, closed Sun

SEVILLA

LA ALBAHACA (€€)
Housed in a typical Andalucían house, decorated with tiles and plants. Spanish and French cuisine.
✉ Plaza Santa Cruz ☎ 954 22 07 14 ⌚ Lunch and dinner, closed Sun

CASA ROBLES (€€)

Traditional restaurant near the cathedral. Classic Andalucian dishes and lively *tapas* bar downstairs, a favourite with locals.

Calle Álvarez Quinters 58 954 56 32 72 Lunch and dinner

EL GIRALDILLO (€€)

Established restaurant with excellent location facing the cathedral and Giralda. Tables out on the pavement for a casual drink and a light meal.

Plaza Virgen de los Reyes 2 954 21 45 25 Lunch and dinner

EL RINCÓN DE PEPE (€€)

Popular restaurant in the Barrio Santa Cruz. Outdoor eating in season.

Calle Gloria 6, Barrio Santo Cruz 954 56 29 75 Lunch and dinner

TORREMOLINOS

LA BODEGA (€)

Located right on the lively Calle San Miguel this place is constantly busy; frequented by locals and tourists.

Calle San Miguel 40 952 38 73 37 Lunch and dinner

EL CHACHA (€)

This open-air seafood *tapas* bar is a Torremolinos institution. Stand to sample its wide range of fresh fish and seafood, offered at very reasonable prices.

✉ Palma de Mallorca 3 ☎ None 🕓 Lunch and dinner

EL COMEDOR (€€)

Stylish establishment in the picturesque Pueblo Blanco quarter. The menu is based on good quality Basque cooking.

✉ Calle Casablanca, Pueblo Blanco ☎ 952 38 38 81 🕓 Lunch and dinner, closed Sat. Weekends only in winter

DONA FRANCISQUITA (€€)

Pleasant restaurant, centrally located, with a high standard of cooking and service.

✉ Calle Casablanca, Edif Zurbarán 11 ☎ 952 37 49 10 🕓 Lunch and dinner

LA JÁBEGA (€€)

This lively restaurant along the promenade serves a good choice of meat, fish and seafood.

✉ Paseo Marítimo, La Carihuela ☎ 952 38 63 75 🕓 Lunch, dinner

MED (€€)

Central restaurant. Cool spohisticated ambience. Emphasis on Mediterranean cuisine. Panoramic views.

✉ La Mercedes 12, 2a Planta ☎ 952 05 88 30 🕒 Lunch and dinner, closed Mon

TAPAS

Tapas bars are a way of life in Spain and a visit to some of these establishments will serve to give a feel of the town. A lively atmosphere is usually provided by local people, who meet regularly for animated conversation over a beer or a chilled fino *sherry*. The choice of *tapas* can range from olives, almonds, *jamón serrano* (cured ham), to *tortilla* slices (Spanish-style omelettes), vegetable dishes, and a selection of fish and seafood dishes, often well laced with garlic.

Porciones denote smaller helpings, while *raciones* are more ample. The bars are open for most of the day to serve drinks and food.

Where to stay...
Costa del Sol & beyond

ALMUÑECAR

CASABLANCA (€)

Moorish-style hotel in a pleasant location. Spacious rooms with views over the sea or the castle and mountains behind.

✉ Plaza San Cristóbal ☎ 958 63 55 59

ANTEQUERA

PARADOR DE ANTEQUERA (€)

Modern building in attractive setting amongst ruins of the Moorish fortress.

✉ García de Olmo s/n ☎ 952 84 02 61; **www.**parador.es

BENALMÁDENA COSTA

LAS ARENAS (€)

Six-floor hotel opposite the Arroyo de la Miel and Bil Bil Castle beaches. Most rooms with sea views and terrace.

✉ Avenida Antonio Machado 22 ☎ 952 56 18 05

TRITON (€€)

Long established hotel set in subtropical gardens, with mountain and sea views. Pools and tennis courts.

✉ Avenida Antonio Machado 29 ☎ 952 44 32 40

CÓRDOBA

MELÍA CÓRDOBA (€€€)

Pleasant and centrally located.

✉ Jardines de la Victoria ☎ 957 29 80 66; **www.**solmelia.com

MEZQUITA (€€)

Housed in an old 16th-century house. Attractive decor, conveniently situated opposite the Mosque.

✉ Plaza Santa Cataline 1 ☎ 957 47 55 85

ESTEPONA

ATALAYA PARK (€€€)

Comfortable and set in attractive gardens facing the beach with sports facilities.

✉ Carretera N340 ☎ 952 88 90 00; **www.**atalaya-park.es

LAS DUNAS BEACH HOTEL & SPA (€€€)

On the beach, between Marbella and Estepona. Tropical gardens, Andalucían-style décor with a Middle Eastern influence. Pool, gourmet restaurant, watersports, riding.

✉ La Boladilla Baja, Ctra de Cádiz, Km 163.5 ☎ 952 79 43 45; www.las-dunas.com

DOBAR (€)

Good location on the seafront. Reasonable rates.

✉ Avenida España 178 ☎ 952 80 06 00

EL PARAÍSO (€€)

Set on a hill with good views of the coast and attractive gardens, surrounded by a golf course. Heated outdoor pool.

✉ Ctra de Cádiz, Km 134 ☎ 952 88 30 00; www.hotelparaisocostadelsol.com

SANTA MARTA (€)

Attractive little hotel with bungalows, situated on the seafront. Shady gardens and pool with bar.

✉ Ctra de Cádiz, Km 167 ☎ 952 88 81 77; www.hotelsantamarta.com

FUENGIROLA

ANGELA (€)

Attractively decorated in a modern Andalucían style on the Paseo Marítimo, within walking distance of the beach. Shops, rail and bus transport are all near by.

✉ Paseo Rey de España s/n ☎ 952 47 52 00

FLORIDA (€€)

One of Fuengirola's earliest hotels, this has a pool in semitropical gardens. Live music and shows in summer.

✉ Paseo Maritimo, s/n ☎ 952 47 61 00

HOSTAL ITALIA (€)

Situated in the centre of town, warm family atmosphere. Good value

✉ Calle de la Cruz 1 ☎ 952 47 41 93

LAS PIRÁMIDES (€€)

Near the beach and town centre. Facilities include a garden and pool, flamenco shows and live music. Golf, mini golf and tennis near by.

✉ Miquel Márquez, 43 ☎ 952 47 06 00

VILLA DE LAREDO (€€)

Pleasant new hotel right on the promenade.

✉ Paseo Marítimo 42 ☎ 952 47 76 89

GRANADA

ALHAMBRA PALACE (€€)

Old traditional favourite with Moorish-style décor. Close to the Alhambra with views of the Sierra Nevada from some rooms.

✉ Calle Peña Partida, 2 ☎ (958) 22 14 68; www.h-alhambrapalace.com

NH INGLATERRA (€)

Pleasant hotel, centrally located, housed in a 19th-century house.

✉ Cetti Meriem 4 ☎ 958 22 15 59

MARBELLA

ANDALUCÍA PLAZA (€€)

Spacious establishment, attractively refurbished, set in gardens, two pools, casino.

✉ Nueva Andalucia (opposite Puerto Banús) ☎ 952 81 20 00

CHAPAS PALACIO DEL SOL (€€€)

Set in lovely pine groves, popular with families, sports and nature lovers. Tennis, mini golf, table tennis offered, with riding, golf and watersports in the locale.

✉ Ctra de Cádiz, Km 198 ☎ 952 83 13 75

EL FUERTE (€€)

Attractive hotel in pleasant gardens. Near the sea and within walking distance of Marbella centre.

✉ Avenida El Fuerte ☎ 952 86 15 00; **www.fuertehoteles.com**

HOTEL FUERTE MIRAMAR-SPA (€€€)

Part of the El Fuerte group, this modern hotel on the seafront has an outdoor heated pool, hydrotherapy centre and good facilities.

✉ Plaza José Luque Manzano s/n ☎ 952 76 84 10; **www.fuertehoteles.com**

LIMA (€€)

Close to the old town and a short walk to the seafront.

✉ Avenida Antonio Belón ☎ 952 77 05 00

MARBELLA CLUB (€€)

Old time favourite, set in lush gardens with swimming pool.

✉ Blvd Príncipe Alfonso de Hohenlohe ☎ 952 82 22 11; www.marbellaclub.com

PUENTE ROMANO (€€€)

Super deluxe village-like complex with landscaped gardens, pool, tennis.

✉ Carretera N340, between Marbella and Puerto Banús ☎ 952 82 09 00; www.puenteromano.com

RIU RINCÓN ANDALUZ (€€)

Attractive hotel complex built in an Andalucían-style pueblo. Near Puerto Banús and close to the sea.

✉ N340 Km 173 ☎ 952 81 15 17

SAN CRISTOBAL (€)

Modest, conveniently situated for Marbella centre.

✉ Ramon y Cajal 3 ☎ 952 77 12 50

MIJAS

HOTEL MIJAS (€)

At the entrance to Mijas, the hotel is set amidst gardens with a pool, offering superb views down to the coast.

✉ Urb Tamisa s/n ☎ 952 48 58 00; www.hotasa.es

MONDA

CASTILLO DE MONDA (€€)

Old castle converted into a hotel by British proprietors. Moorish-style furnishings, stunning views of Monda and the Sierra de las Nieves.

✉ Monda (18km northeast of Marbella) ☎ 952 45 71 42; www.costadelsol.spa.es

NERJA

BALCÓN DE EUROPA (€€)

Old favourite located on the promenade of the same name. Private beach.

✉ Paseo Balcón de Europa ☎ 952 52 08 00

PARADOR DE NERJA (€€)

Modern *parador* set high up with pleasant gardens. Splendid views of the beach below and surrounding bay.

✉ Almuñécar 8 ☎ 952 52 00 50; **www.**parador.es

VILLA FLAMENCA (€)

In the Nueva Nerja development, some 300m from the beach, with a garden and pool, restaurant and bar.

✉ Urb. Nueva Nerja ☎ 952 52 21 96

RONDA

MAESTRANZA (€€)

Situated in the centre of town, facing Ronda's old bullring, this hotel has comfortable rooms and tasteful decor. Use of a private country club (tennis, swimming pool, squash).

✉ Calle Virgen de la Paz ☎ 952 18 70 72

REINA VICTORIA (€€)

An old favourite, built in the early 20th century. Set in attractive gardens with swimming pool. Fine views of surrounding mountains.

✉ Calle Jerez 25 ☎ 952 87 12 40; **www.**ronda.net/usuar/victoria

SAN GABRIEL–SU CASA EN RONDA (€€)

Delightful hotel with tasteful decor, housed in an 18th-century mansion with an attractive courtyard.

✉ Marqués de Moctezuma 19 ☎ 952 19 03 92; www.hotelsangabriel.com

SAN PEDRO DE ALCÁNTARA

PUEBLO ANDALUZ (€€)

Built in typical Andalucían style with a pool and gardens.

✉ Avenida Luis Carillo Benítez ☎ 952 78 05 97

SEVILLA

ALFONSO XIII (€€€)

One of Spain's most famous hotels. Built around a large courtyard with arches and plenty of greenery. Unique Moorish-style with magnificent marble floors and panelled ceilings.

✉ Calle San Fernando 2 ☎ 954 22 28 50

BÉCQUER (€)

Pleasant establishment. Good location, near the town centre and the river.

✉ Calle Reyes Católicos 4 ☎ 954 22 89 00; www.hotelbecquer.com

HOSTERÍA DEL LAUREL (€€)

In the heart of the picturesque Barrio de Santa Cruz. Has an outdoor restaurant in a square lined with pretty houses.

✉ Plaza de los Venerables 5 ☎ 954 22 02 95

HOTEL AMADEUS (€€)

Small hotel of great charm, with attractive decor and character. Will appeal to music lovers. Family run, warm and welcoming.

✉ Calle Farnesio 6 ☎ 954 50 14 43

TORREMOLINOS

CERVANTES (€€)

Large hotel a few minutes' walk from town centre. Garden with pool, rooftop pool, restaurant, casino. Live music and dancing. Undergoing extensive refurbishment at time of writing.

✉ Calle Las Mercedes s/n ☎ 952 38 40 33; www.hotelcervantestorremolinos.es

FÉNIX (€€)

In the centre of town, with direct access to the beach. Garden and pool, sauna, gymnasium and evening entertainment.

✉ Las Mercedes 24 ☎ 952 37 52 68

HOSTAL LOS RISCOS (€)

Small and friendly with rooms and apartments, in a quiet residential area, near the town centre. English speaking personnel.

✉ Calle Loma de los Riscos 40 ☎ 952 37 21 99

PEZ ESPADA (€€€)

This large hotel offers all comforts, with a swimming pool surrounded by gardens.

✉ Vía Imperial 11, La Carihuela ☎ 952 38 03 00;
www.medplaya.com

TROPICANA HOTEL AND BEACH CLUB (€€€)

Colourful tropical design and layout. Kidney-shaped pool set in gardens and beach club add to its appeal.

✉ Calle Trópico 6, La Carihuela ☎ 952 38 66 00;
www.hotel-tropicana.net.reservas

SHOPPING

ANTIQUE SHOPS

GRANADA

GONZÁLO REYES MUÑOZ

✉ Calle Mesones (Placeta de Cauchiles 1) ☎ 958 52 32 74

MÁLAGA

A VELA DÍAZ

✉ San Augustín 10 ☎ 952 21 25 28

E RUIZ LINARES

✉ Santa Maria 21 ☎ 952 22 80 47

EL MARTINETE

✉ Carretería 90 ☎ 952 21 33 35

EL TRIANON

✉ Madre de Dios 22 ☎ 952 21 08 46

RONDA

EL PORTÓN

Manuel Montero 14 952 87 24 10

MUÑOZ SOTO

B S Juan de Dios de Córdoba 34 952 87 14 51

SAN PEDRO DE ALCÁNTARA

CABON S L ANTIGUEDADES

Large showroom offering an extensive range of attractive Spanish and Portugese rustic antique furniture.

Ctra de Cádiz, Lm 169.5, Guadalmina Baja 952 88 28 97

BOOKSTORES

NERJA

NERJA BOOK CENTRE

Large secondhand book store, stocking thousands of books in several different languages.

Calle Granda 30 952 52 09 08

CERAMICS

ESTEPONA

CERÁMICA LA CHIMINEA

Beautiful designs created by Paco Leonicio, who learnt his crafts at Triana, one of Spain's top centres for pottery. Wide selection of decorative tiles, glazed and unglazed ceramics.

✉ Ctra Cádiz–Málaga, Km 162.2 ☎ 952 79 44 75

MÁLAGA

CERÁMICA FINA

Cerámica Fina stocks attractively displayed ceramics of all kinds showing a high standard of workmanship.

✉ Calle Coronel 5, near the church of San Juan ☎ No phone available

SAN PEDRO DE ALCÁNTARA

ARTESANÍA TROYANO

Specialists in porcelain, features Lladró porcelain and other fine makes.

✉ Calle Lagasca 63. Also in Marqués del Duero ☎ 952 78 11 99

SEVILLA

SEVILLARTE

A wide range of beautiful ceramic products at three branches.

✉ Branches at: Gloria 5 ☎ 954 21 88 35; Sierpes 66 ☎ 954 21 28 36; Vida 13 ☎ 954 56 29 45

FASHION

FUENGIROLA

BRANDTEX

Ladies' boutique with stylish fashionware available in all sizes. Good selection of mix and match outfits.

✉ Avenida Suel 4, Edificio Tres Coronas ☎ 952 58 25 85

MÁLAGA

BOUTIQUE AZULAY

Good selection of high quality fashionwear.

✉ Larios 10 ☎ 952 21 75 39

MANGO

One branch of Spain's well-known chain of elegant fashion stores.

✉ Larios 1 ☎ 952 22 31 02

MARBELLA

DON MIGUEL

Long established, with wide range of fashionwear for men and women. Some of the brand names to be found here.

✉ Avenida Ricardo Soriano 5 ☎ 952 77 31 40

GUCCI

No introduction needed. Elegant range of men's and women's clothing.

✉ Calle Valdéz 8 ☎ 952 86 14 99

LOUIS FERAUD

Fashion clothes by Feraud, known for their striking designs and vibrant colours.

✉ Plaza Victoria ☎ 952 82 81 06

NERJA

BRUNA CAVVALINI

Some good bargains may be had in this fashionable ladies' boutique. Sportswear and more formal gear available, plus accessories. Clothes from Sevilla and London.

✉ Calle Barrio ☎ 952 52 30 58

MOSTAZA

Casual and formal wear . Shirts, sweaters, suits and jackets.

✉ Calle Diputación Provincial 6 ☎ 952 52 14 00

PUERTO BANÚS

BOUTIQUE DONNA PIU

Italian-style fashion.

✉ Paseo Benabola L87 ☎ 952 81 49 90

BOUTIQUE NUMBER ONE

Specialises in French and Italian designer collections.

✉ Levante 1 ☎ 952 81 16 97

GIANNI VERSACE

Ideal for the fashion conscious, men's and women's fashions.

✉ Centro Comercial Benabola 8 ☎ 952 81 02 96

TORRE DEL MAR

SINGH

Elegant boutique for women's and men's clothes. Top fashion names, with the latest designs.

✉ Calle Avenida de Andalucía 121 ☎ 952 54 10 91

FOOD AND WINE SHOPS

PUERTO BANÚS

CLUB DE GOURMET

Exciting range of unusual products. Next to Bar Inglés.

✉ By entrance to Puerto Banús, near El Corte Inglés ☎ 952 81 78 00

SAN PEDRO ALCÁNTARA

ANDRÉS INGELMO MARCOS

Quality Iberian ham and sausages. Cheeses and Rioja wines.

✉ c/ Miguel Hernández 4 ☎ 952 78 65 56

GIFT SHOPS

BENALMÁDENA (PUERTO MARINA)

LA MAISON

Ideal for small gifts such as porcelain and ceramic fish.

✉ Puerto Marina ☎ 952 56 0299

FUENGIROLA

REGALOS DE ARTE MAXI

Attractive choice of Lladró porcelain, ceramics from Sevilla, Majorcan pearls and a good selection of easy to carry gifts.

✉ Avenida Ramón y Cajal 1 ☎ 952 47 33 34

MÁLAGA

ORIGINAL

A variety of gifts made in wood, including reproductions of music boxes and antique toys.

✉ Calle Caldería 2, and Calle Marín García 6 ☎ None

MARBELLA

DUPAR

Local distributors of Lladró and Majorica. Wide range of gifts.

✉ Avenida Ramón y Cajal 3 ☎ None

TORREMOLINOS

LAS TRES TORRES

Offers a good choice of products, including a wide range of items made in Toledo steel, ceramics and pottery from Sevilla, and an attractive selection of Majorcan pearls.

✉ Calle San Miguel 17 ☎ 952 21 79 39

MONTINAS GIFT SHOP

A wide variety of attractive gifts available. Official agents for Lladró, Majorica and Swarovski.

✉ La Nogalera 26 ☎ 952 38 11 78

JEWELLERY

FUENGIROLA

NICHOLSON

Modern jewellery designs. Also in Marbella's Orange Square.

✉ Calle Marbella s/n ☎ 952 47 58 82

MARBELLA

JOYERÍA DON LAL

Extensive selection of jewellery. Branches in Puerto Banús, Ribera 167, Casa OPQ and Torremolinos, San Miguel 48.

✉ Avenida Ramón y Cajal 3 ☎ 952 86 66 53

SAN PEDRO DE ALCÁNTARA

ANTHONY'S JEWELLERS

Unusual and original designs by the owner, with many pieces incorporating semi-precious stones.

✉ Plaza las Faroles ☎ 952 78 62 74

TORREMOLINOS

JOYERÍA SAN MIGUEL

Good selection of all types of jewellery and watches.

✉ San Miguel 11 ☎ 952 38 05 53

LEATHERWARE

BENALMÁDENA

ARTESANÍA PIEL

Leather goods produced on the premises. Out of the ordinary belts and handicrafts.

✉ Puerto Marina ☎ None

FUENGIROLA

BRAVO

Good reputation for shoes, handbags, luggage and leather accessories. Shops also in Marbella and Torremolinos.

✉ Avenida Condes de San Isidro 33 ☎ 952 46 17 19

MÁLAGA

NUÑEZ ANTILOPE

An old leather factory stocking suede and leather gear.

✉ Bolsa s/n ☎ 952 21 27 45

MARBELLA

CHARLES JOURDAN

Wide range of shoes and leather goods.

✉ Avenida Ramón y Cajal ☎ 952 77 00 03

STORES

MÁLAGA

EL CORTE INGLÉS

Six floors of fashion, gifts, exhibitions of arts and crafts.

✉ Avenida de Andalucia 4–6 ☎ 952 30 00 00

MÁLAGA PLAZA CENTRO COMERCIAL

American-style complex with a variety of quality shops.

✉ Armengual de la Mota 12 ☎ 952 61 40 40

MARBELLA

LA CAÑADA COMMERCIAL CENTRE

Centre with individual shops and a supermarket.

✉ Parque Comerical la Cañada, Ctra de Ojén s/n ☎ 952 86 01 42

PUERTO BANÚS

COSTA MARBELLA DEPARTMENT STORE

Gigantic superstore, just outside town. Part of the El Corte chain, with a hypermarket (Hipercor) on the ground floor and specialised shops on the upper floors.

✉ Ctra N340, Km 174 ☎ 952 90 99 90

NIGHTLIFE

CASINOS

BENALMÁDENA COSTA

CASINO TORREQUEBRADA

Roulette, blackjack, Punto Blanco, slot machines and private gaming room. Dress is formal and passports must be shown.

Avenida del Sol s/n 952 44 60 00 Daily 8pm–4am Bus stop Benalmádena Costa Expensive

NUEVA ANDALUCÍA

CASINO MARBELLA

American and French roulette, blackjack, Stud Caribbean poker, slot machines. Jacket and tie for men. Passport required.

Hotel Andalucía Plaza, opposite Puerto Banus, Nueva Andalucía 952 81 40 00 Daily 9pm–3am Bus stop Andalucía Plaza Expensive

CASINO NUEVA SAN ROQUE

Chic casino offering roulette and blackjack. Passport, jacket and tie required.

Ctra N340, Km127 965 78 10 00

CINEMA AND THEATRE

Among the various cinemas and theatres along the coast, which can be enjoyed by locals and visitors alike, one place stands out as a rock of entertainment for the English-speaking community in the area. The Salon Varietés, which first opened in Fuengirola in 1985, continues to put on a variety of entertainment each season, which is from the middle of September to mid-June. Audiences can enjoy all types of plays, from thrillers to comedies, musicals and pantomines, concerts, flamenco shows and dance festivals, and lectures.

FUENGIROLA

CINE SOHAIL

✉ Avenida Condes de San Isidro s/n ☎ 952 47 46 41

SALON VARIÉTÉS

Cinema and theatre with regular plays and entertainment for the English-speaking community.

✉ Emancipacón 30 ☎ 952 47 45 42

MÁLAGA

ALAMEDA MULTICINES
✉ Córdoba 13 ☎ 952 21 34 12

ALBEÑIZ MULTICINES
✉ Alcazabilla 4 ☎ 952 21 58 98

AMÉRICA MULTICINES
✉ Explanada de la Estación ☎ 952 33 99 91

ANDALUCÍA CINEMA
✉ Victoria 2 ☎ 952 21 06 16

ASTORIA CINEMA
✉ Plaza de Maria Guerrero ☎ 952 21 20 64

ECHEGARAY CINEMA
✉ Echegaray 13 ☎ 952 21 39 99

SALA CÁNOVAS
Plays, opera and concerts are performed here in winter with

the Málaga Symphony Orchestra.
✉ Plaza del Ejido s/n ☎ 952 25 72 00

TEATRO MIGUEL DE CERVANTES
Major cultural centre with year round programme.
✉ Ramos Martín s/n ☎ 952 22 41 00

PUERTO BANÚS

CINE GRAN MARBELLA
You can often see films in English at this multiplex.
✉ Puerto Banús ☎ 952 81 00 77

SEVILLA

TEATRO MUNICIPAL ALAMEDA
Varied programme of plays.
✉ Calle Crédito 13 ☎ 954 90 01 62

TEATRO LOPE DE VEGA
For classical concerts.
✉ Avenida María Luisa s/n ☎ 954 59 08 53

FLAMENCO AND JAZZ

Flamenco is closely associated with Andalucía, where its roots belong. For the visitor who wishes to get the flavour of something seen as 'typically Spanish' there are plenty of nightspots along the Costa with flamenco shows which can be colourful and entertaining. The real magic of flamenco, however, is spontaneity and the right ambience, which is not so easy to find. You could experience some good flamenco at a local fiesta, or tucked away in the back streets of towns such as Sevilla or Málaga accompanied, ideally, by someone who knows where to look.

Jazz fans have plenty of opportunities to indulge their interest as numerous cafés and piano bars in the main resorts, in particular Torremolinos, Fuengirola, Marbella and Puerto Banús, offer live music which can include jazz, blues and soul. Concerts are also laid on for visiting musicians. These take place in a clubs and some of the hotels along the coast.

The Mississippi-style paddleboat *Willow*, moored in the bay of Puerto Marina Benalmádena, holds jazz concerts by international artists, in addition to regular performances of their own 'resident' Willow Dixieland Band. Enthusiasts can check with local newspapers for a programme of events.

DANCE CLUBS

FUENGIROLA

DISCOTECA SUPERSTAR

✉ Calle Jacinto Benavente s/n ☎ 952 47 04 92

MÁLAGA

VARSOVIA

Popular with all age groups.

✉ Calle José Denis Belgrado 5 ☎ No phone

PIANO CLUB GEORGES

✉ Mar 90 ☎ 952 22 82 39

SURF

✉ Calle S Nicolás 2 ☎ 952 22 74 83

MARBELLA

DISCO WILLY SALSA

Popular with the younger set.

✉ Ctra Cádiz, Km 178 ☎ 952 82 73 63

OH! MARBELLA

A real hot spots, with good views from the terrace.

✉ Hotel Don Carlos, Ctra de Cádiz, Km 192 ☎ 952 83 54 77

OLIVIA VALERE

A Costa del Sol favourite. Passport required.

✉ Ctra de Istán, Km 0.8 ☎ 952 82 88 45

TORREMOLINOS

NEW MARIO

Favoured by an older set.

✉ Calle Casablanca ☎ 952 37 50 37 🕐 Closed Mon

PALLADIUM

A popular spot, with trendy lighting and loud music.

✉ Avenida Palma de Mallorca 36 ☎ 952 38 42 89

PIPER DISCOTECA

Funky music, young crowd.

✉ Avenida de Mallorca ☎ No phone 🕐 Closed Mon

SPORT

Along the Costa del Sol bullfights are held on Sunday afternoons during the summer season in Málaga, Estepona and Marbella. The bigger names, however, are attracted by Sevilla, Córdoba and other prominent towns in Andalucía.

Other spectator sports include soccer, basketball, tennis and golf, including the World Cup, the Spanish and the Ryder cups. Polo matches are held in Sotogrande from July to September. Check with local publications for information.

ADVENTURE ACTIVITIES

Explore the hinterland by jeep on a day's mini-safari, which will take you over mountainous terrain, and through parklands.

BORN TO BE WILD ADVENTURES (ECO TOURS)
Nature tours by jeep, designed for the whole family to enjoy together.
✉ Marbella ☎ 639 72 02 56

MARBELLA RANGERS JEEP SAFARIS
☎ 952 83 30 82

BIKING

Explore the countryside by bicycle, mountain bike, moped or motorbike. Routes recommended if required.

MOTOMERCADO

✉ Calle Sant Rosa 18, Los Boliches, Fuengirola ☎ 952 47 25 51. Branches in Torremolinos, Benalmádena and Marbella.

IN THE AIR

AVIACIÓN DEL SOL

Hot-air balloon trips offering spectacular views of the Serranía de Ronda. Departure just after dawn, four passengers only.

✉ Ronda–Servilla (A376), Km 114.5 ☎ 952 87 72 49

These two clubs near Málaga offer hang-gliding and paragliding courses for beginners; tandem flights with an instructor.

CLUB ESCUELA PARAPENTE EL VALLE

✉ Valle de Abdalajís ☎ 952 48 91 80

CLUB VUELO LIBRE MÁLAGA

✉ Valle de Abdalajís ☎ 952 48 92 98

FLYSURFING

Good spots for flysurfing, or kitesurfing are in Torrox, Chilches, Málaga (El Palo and El Candado), Guadalmar, Los Alamos and Playamar, between Málaga and Torremolinos, Benalmádena, Mijas Costa (El Chaparral, La Cale, Cabo Pino), Marbella (El Rosario, Guadalmina) and Estepona or Manilva's beaches.

ANDALUCIAN AERIEL SPORTS FEDERATION

☎ 952 60 13 61.

GOLF

Green fees for golf courses on the Costa del Sol are considered to be amongst the most competitive in Europe. Many hotels also offer their guests reduced green fees. The majority of golf clubs require a handicap certificate. Courses get booked up by members so visitors are advised to book well in advance. Useful publications include:

Golf in Andalucía ✉ Calle Calvario 8, Marbella ☎ 952 82 89 76 **Revista Costa Golf** ✉ Apartado Correos 358, Torremolinos. **The Federación Andaluza de Golf** ✉ Calle Sierra de Grazalema 33, bloque 5, 29016 Málaga ☎ 952 22 55 99/90

HORSERIDING

ESTEPONA

FINCA SIESTA

Offers picnic and beach rides as well as a range of lessons in dressage and showjumping.

✉ Km 163 on N230 (opposite Hacienda Beach) ☎ 952 79 01 89

MARBELLA

CLUB HÍPICO ELVIRIA

✉ El Platero, between Marbella and Fuengirola ☎ 952 83 52 72

MARBELLA CLUB HOTEL

A new equestrian centre, offering lessons and rides.

✉ Boulevard Principe Alfonso de Hohenlohe ☎ 952 82 98 84

LOS MONTEROS HOTEL

Provides lessons and rides taking in the surrounding hills.

✉ Ctra de Cádiz, N340, Km 177 ☎ 952 11 25 53

SAN PEDRO DE ALCÁNTARA

LAKEVIEW EQUESTRIAN CENTRE

Qualified instruction in dressage and showjumping; private or

group lessons.
✉ Valle del Sol ☎ 952 78 69 34

SAN ROQUE

THE SAN ROQUE CLUB EQUESTRIAN CENTRE

For beginners and experienced riders. One hour or full day hacks.
✉ San Roque Club Suites Hotel, Ctra Cádiz, Km 126.5 ☎ 956 61 32 32

SOTOGRANDE POLO

You can experience the thrill of riding top class polo ponies on Sotogrande's polo fields.
☎ 956 79 64 64

TORRE DEL MAR

LAVAO VILLALBA

✉ ✋ Ctra V Alméria s/n ☎ 952 54 14 43

TORREMOLINOS

HÍPICA INTERNATIONAL

Lessons in dressage and jumping. One hour hacks for

experienced riders (2,000 ptas). Refreshments available.
✉ Camino de la Sierra ☎ 952 43 55 49

GONZÁLEZ-GARRIDO

✉ ✋ Ctra de Cádiz s/n
☎ 952 38 30 63

CLUB EL RANCHITO

Full horse riding facilities available (➤ 107).
✉ Camino del Pilar, La Colima ☎ 952 38 31 40

For futher information about horse riding in rural Andalucia contact: **Asociación de Empresarios de Turismo Equestre de Andalucía (AETEA)**
✉ Isla de la Cartuja s/n, 41092 Servilla ☎ 954 46 00 01

TENNIS

Most top hotels along the coast have tennis courts, especially in and around Marbella. Hotel guests have priority in renting the courts. There are also a number of tennis clubs in the area.

WATERSPORTS

SAILING

The major marinas dotted along the coast have excellent sailing facilities. Most of the marinas and their yacht clubs organise beginners' sailing, monitor and yacht-master classes in summer. Major marinas and yacht clubs include:

La Duqesa ☎ 952 89 01 00, Estepona ☎ 952 80 18 00, Marbella ☎ 952 77 57 00, Fuengirola ☎ 952 46 80 00, Benalmádena ☎ 952 44 30 48, Málaga ☎ 952 22 63 00

SCUBA DIVING

Almuñecar and Nerja, east of Málaga, are good centres for diving. Day courses with qualified instructors are available at:

CENTRO BUCEO TARIFA

✉ Calle Alcalde Juan Nuñez 10 ☎ 956 68 16 48

CLUB NAUTICO DIVING CENTRE

✉ Puerto Marina de Benalmádena ☎ 952 56 07 69

FUENGIROLA DIVING CENTRE

✉ Fuengirola port ☎ 952 58 83 12

SWIMMING

The beaches of the Costa del Sol vary from sand to fine grit and shingle. Some of the best sandy beaches are around Torremolinos, Fuengirola and on either side of Marbella, all of which can become very crowded in the summer season. For more secluded beaches try the coast east of Málaga or west of Estepona.

WATERSKIING AND WINDSURFING

There are plenty of opportunities for waterskiing and windsurfing along the western coast of Costa del Sol. Facilities and tuition are available in all major resorts, often from the hotels. The top spot for windsurfing is at Tarifa, where strong winds provide favourable conditions.

AKY OKAPY

✉ Calle Ave María 7, Tarifa ☎ 956 68 53 56

CLUB MISTRAL

Wind boards for rent on the beach. Lessons available.

✉ Hotel Hurricane, Tarifa Ctra N340, Km 77 ☎ 952 68 49 19

TAKE THE CHILDREN

BENALMÁDENA

SELWO MARINA

This new type of marina/fauna park contains Andalucía's first dolphinarium and penguinarium. Exhibitions feature dolphins, sea lions and exotic birds. 3D cinemas and a children's playground offer plenty of fun all round.

✉ Parque de la Paloma s/n Benalmádena ☎ 902 19 04 82
🕐 Daily 10–6 ✋ Moderate

TIVOLI WORLD, ARROYO DE LA MIEL

This show and amusement park, set in extensive grounds, is a great favourite with families, especially at the weekend. In addition to numerous rides and amusements (including a giant rollercoaster), visitors can enjoy flamenco shows, a Wild West Town, theatre and live music. Tivolilandia is an infant area, and Tivoli Agua, contains a water mountain flume ride.

✉ Avenida de Tivoli s/n ☎ 952 57 70 16 🕐 Apr, May, 15–30 Sep, Oct daily 4pm–1am; Jun, 1–14 Sep 5pm–2am; Jul– Aug 6pm–3am; Nov–Mar 11am–9pm (times subject to change) ✋ Moderate
🚆 RENFE station Arroyo de la Miel 🚌 Arroyo de la Miel

BENALMÁDENA COSTA

SEA LIFE BENALMÁDENA

This sea life centre takes you on an exciting voyage of discovery to the bottom of the ocean. From the shallow waters to the depths of the sea you can enjoy close views of a whole wealth of marine life, ranging from tiny shrimps and starfish to giant stingrays and great sharks. There are also presentations and feeding displays. An area dedicated to the sea horse is a delightful new addition.

Puerto Deportivo, Benalmádena 952 56 01 50 D Daily 10–6 Moderate Restaurant (€€) RENFE station Benalmádena Good

BANALMÁDENA PUEBLO

JARDÍN DE LAS AGUÍLAS (EAGLE GARDENS)

Up the hill, in the Castillo de Aguílas, is the Birds of Prey Centre, where demonstrations are held with eagles, owls, falcons and vultures. Next door is a miniature castle, Castillo Colombo, and a reptile sanctuary, Snake City.

Castillo de Aguílas just before Benalmádena Pueblo 952 56 82 39 Show times daily: Oct–Apr, 1, 5; May–Jun, 1, 6, 7, 8; Jul, Aug, 1, 6, 8 subject to weather Moderate Bus to Benalmádena Pueblo

ESTEPONA

SELWO AVENTURA

A safari park where you can see a whole range of animals from the five continents of the world, roaming around in a semi-wild habitat. Much of the circuit is made by truck.

Autovía Costa del Sol, Km 162.5, Las Lomas del Monte 902 19 04 82 Jan–May, Oct–Dec daily 10–6; Jun–Sep 10–7 Moderate Direct to Selwo (Costa line)

FUENGIROLA

ZOO FUENGIROLA

Spectacular modern new zoo, designed to re-create the natural habitat of all the species living here. Wander among tropical forests, rivers and waterfalls to glimpse its varied flora and fauna, including chimpanzees, crocodiles, numerous birds and reptiles. Restaurants and a children's area all contribute to a wonderful family outing.

Camolio José Cela, 6 Fuengirola 952 66 63 01 Daily 10–6 Moderate RENFE station Fuengirola

MARBELLA

FUNNY BEACH MARBELLA

Family leisure centre offering mostly water activities, including go-kart races, water bikes, 'ski' banana, quad trips.

Ctra. Cádiz, 340 Marbella 952 82 33 59 Daily 11–11 Free

MIJAS COSTA

PARQUE ACUÁTICO MIJAS (AQUALAND)

This water theme park has great watershoots, including a thrilling Kamikaze, pools, slides and rapids.

Ctra N340, Km 290 952 46 04 09 May, daily 10– 5:30; Jun, Sep 10–6; Jul, Aug 10–7; closed Oct–Apr Expensive Restaurant (€€) Fuengirola bus station Few

PUERTO BANÚS

SUPER BONANZA

The *Bonanza* departs every two hours from midday onwards for a cruise along the coast.

Sinatra Bar, Puerto Banús 952 38 55 00

TORRE DEL MAR

PARQUE ACUÁTICO AQUAVELIS

Another fun water park that the children will enjoy.

Urb El Tomillar 952 54 25 92 Daily 10–6 Moderate
Bus from Málaga (Torre del Mar stop)

TORREMOLINOS

AQUAPARK

Aquatic attractions here include giant water chutes, water mountains and artificial waves bearing names such as Kamikaze, Cresta Run and Waikiki Surf. The Aquapark also boasts a mini park, restaurant and boutique.

Ctra de Circunvalación (near Palacio de Congresos) 952 38 88 88 Jul–Sep daily 10–6, Dec–Feb 10–5 JModerate Restaurant
RENFE station Torremolinos

CROCODILE PARK

Centrally located in Torremolinos, the park features more than 300 crocodiles of all ages and sizes, which can be viewed at close quarters. Guided visits with a crocodile trainer available.

Calle Cuba, 14 Torremolinas C952 05 17 82 Shows: Wed 5:30, Jun–Oct 6 Expensive Nearby Nearby

WHAT'S ON WHEN

JANUARY

Los Reyes Magos (6 January). In Málaga. The Three Kings throw sweets to children from grand floats.

FEBRUARY/MARCH

Carnaval (the week before Lent). In Málaga, Granada and Antequera. An exuberant affair with floats, colourful costumes, music and dancing.

MARCH/APRIL

Semana Santa (Holy Week, moveable date). In Sevilla, Málaga and Granada. From Palm Sunday to Easter Day there are nightly processions of *cofradías* (brotherhoods) carrying images of the saints or the Virgin; wearing pointed hoods, each carries a lighted candle. The muffled drums are accompanied by the occasional *saeta* (an improvised religious lament).

APRIL

Fería de Sevilla (Seville Fair). Originally a cattle fair, the Fair has evolved into a world famous event of colour, music and dancing. The daily horseback parade is a special attraction with the men in dashing outfits, and their ladies in traditional flamboyant dresses. Every afternoon bullfights take place in the Maestranza ring with the most famous of Spain's matadors.

MAY

Las Cruces de Mayo (early May). This represents an ancient custom when crosses decorated with both real and paper flowers are placed in the streets and squares. The fiesta is particularly attractive in Torrox and Coín.

MAY/JUNE

Corpus Christi (moveable date). Processions along flower strewn streets. Especially colourful in Granada, with parades, music and dancing.

JULY

La Virgen del Carmen (16 July). Most spectacualr at Los Boliches, Fuengirola; also at Estepona, Marbella and Nerja. The patron saint of fishermen is paraded through the streets before being taken around the bay on a boat; fireworks, music and dancing on the beach.

SEPTEMBER

Pedro Romero Fiestas (early September). Ronda celebrates the bullfighter with *corridas Goyescas* (Goya-style bullfights), with top matadors in the costume of Goya's time.

OCTOBER

Feria del Rosario. This fair is celebrated in Fuengirola during the first two weeks in October. *Casetas* (clubhouses) of various societies and brotherhoods set up between Fuengirola and Los Boliches offer shows, food and drink. A lively affair, with horse-riding events, flamenco and fireworks.

DECEMBER

Fiesta de Verdiales (29 December). In La Venta de San Cayetano, in Puerto de la Torre, Málaga. Colourfully attired *pandas* (musical groups) compete with each other; a lively event with music, food and wine.

Preferente
PREFERENTE
Coche 03

Language guide

Spanish is one of the easiest languages. All vowels are pure and short (as in English). Some useful tips on speaking: 'c' is lisped before 'e' and 'i', otherwise hard; 'h' is silent; 'j' is pronounced like a gutteral 'j'; 'r' is rolled; 'v' sounds more like 'b'; and 'z' is the same as a soft 'c'. English is widely spoken in the principal resorts but you will get a better reception if you at least try communicating with Spaniards in their own tongue.

More extensive coverage can be found in the AA's *Essential Spanish Phrase Book* which lists over 2,000 phrases and 2,000 words.

hotel	**hotel**
room	**habitación**
single	**individual**
double one	**doble una**
two nights	**dos noche(s)**
per person	**por persona**
per room	**por habitación**
reservation	**reserva**
rate	**precio**
breakfast	**desayuno**
toilet	**lavabo**
bath	**baño**
shower	**ducha**
en suite	**en su habitación**
balcony	**balcón**
key	**llave**
chambermaid	**camarera**

bank	**banco**
exchange office	**oficina de cambio**
post office	**correos**
cashier	**cajero**
money	**dinero**
coin	**moneda**
foreign currency	**moneda extranjera**
change money	**cambiar dinero**
pound sterling	**libra esterlina**
American dollar	**dólar estadounidense**
bank card	**tarjeta del banco**
credit card	**tarjeta de crédito**
giro bank card	**tarjeta de la caja postal**
cheque	**cheque**
traveller's cheque	**cheque de viajero**
giro cheque	**cheque postal**

restaurant	**restaurante**
bar	**bar**
table	**mesa**
menu	**carta**
tourist menu	**menú turístico**
wine list	**carta de vinos**
lunch	**almuerzo**
dinner	**cena**
snack	**merienda**
starter	**primer plato**
dish	**plato**
main course	**plato principal**
dessert	**postre**
drink	**bebida**
waiter	**camarero**
bill	**cuenta**

aeroplane	**avión**
airport	**aeropuerto**
train… station	**tren estación de ferrocarril**
bus… station	**autobús estación de autobuses**
… stop	**parada de autobús**
ferry	**transbordador**
port	**puerto**
ticket	**billete**
… single/return	**ida/ida y vuelta**
… first-/second-class	**primera/segunda clase**
timetable	**horario**
seat	**asiento**
non-smoking	**no fumadore**

yes	**sí**
no	**no**
please	**por favor**
thank you	**gracias**
hello	**hola**
goodbye	**adiós**
good night	**buenas noches**
excuse me	**perdóneme**
help!	**ayuda!**
today	**hoy**
tomorrow	**mañana**
yesterday	**ayer**
how much?	**¿cuánto?**
expensive	**caro**
open	**abierto**
closed	**cerrado**

Practicalities

WHAT YOU NEED

● Required
○ Suggested
▲ Not required

Some countries require a passport to remain valid for a minimum period (usually at least six months) beyond the date of entry – contact their consulate or embassy or your travel agent for details.

	UK	Germany	USA	Netherlands
Passport/National Identity Card	●	●	●	●
Visa (regulations can change – check before your journey)	▲	▲	▲	▲
Onward or Return Ticket	●	●	●	●
Health Inoculations	▲	▲	▲	▲
Health Documentation (reciprocal agreement document, ➤ 248, Health)	▲	▲	▲	▲
Travel Insurance	○	○	○	○
Driving Licence (national – EU format/national/Spanish trnsltn/interntnal)	●	●	●	●
Car Insurance Certificate (if own car)	●	●	●	●
Car Registration Document (if own car)	●	●	●	●

TOURIST OFFICES

In the UK

Spanish Tourist Office,
22/23 Manchester Square,
London W1U 3PX
☎ (020) 7486 8077
Fax: (020) 7486 8034

In the USA

Tourist Office of Spain,
666 Fifth Avenue 35th,
New York, NY 10103
☎ (212) 265 8822
Fax: (212) 265 8864

Tourist Office of Spain,
8383 Wilshire Boulevard,
Suite 960,
Beverley Hills, Cal 90211
☎ (323) 658 7188
Fax: (323) 658 1061

CUSTOMS

YES

From another EU country for personal use (guidelines)

800 cigarettes, 200 cigars,
1 kilogram of tobacco
10 litres of spirits (over 22%)
20 litres of aperitifs
90 litres of wine, of which 60 litres can be sparkling wine
110 litres of beer

From a non-EU country for your personal use, the allowances are:

200 cigarettes OR
50 cigars OR
250 grams of tobacco
1 litre of spirits (over 22%)
2 litres of intermediary products (eg sherry) and sparkling wine
2 litres of still wine
50 grams of perfume
0.25 litres of eau de toilette
The value limit for goods is 175 euros

Travellers under 17 years of age are not entitled to the tobacco and alcohol allowances.

NO

Drugs, firearms, ammunition, offensive weapons, obscene material, unlicensed animals.

WHEN TO GO

Average temperatures for Costa del Sol

High season

Low season

JAN	FEB	MAR	APR	MAY	JUN	JUL	AUG	SEP	OCT	NOV	DEC
Low season	Low season	Low season	High season	High season	High season	High season	High season	High season	Low season	Low season	Low season
16°C	17°C	18°C	21°C	23°C	27°C	29°C	29°C	27°C	23°C	19°C	17°C

Very wet   Wet   Cloud   Sun   Sunshine & showers

ARRIVING

Most visitors to the Costa del Sol arrive at Málaga Airport (☎ 952 04 88 04). Spain's national airline, Iberia (☎ 302 40 05 00), operates direct scheduled flights to Málaga from major European and North American cities. The other nearest airport is Seville.

Málaga Airport

10km to city centre

Journey times

12 minutes

20 minutes

20 minutes

Seville Airport

8km to city centre

Journey times

N/A

20 minutes

20 minutes

MONEY

The euro is the single currency of the European Monetary Union, which has been adopted by 12 member states including Spain. Euro banknotes and coins were introduced in January 2002. There are banknotes for 5, 10, 20, 50, 100, 200 and 500 euros, and coins for 1, 2, 5, 10, 20 and 50 cents, and 1 and 2 euros. Euro traveller's cheques are widely accepted. Spain's former currency, the peseta, went out of circulation in February 2002.

€10

€50

€100

€200

TIME

Spain is one hour ahead of Greenwich Mean Time (GMT+1), but from late March until the Saturday before the last Sunday in October, summer time (GMT+2) operates.

TOURIST OFFICES

Costa del Sol

Costa del Sol Tourist Board
☎ 952 05 86 94/95
www.visitacostadelsol.com

Towns/Resorts

Plaza San Sebastian 7, Antequera
☎ 952 70 25 05

Avenida Antonio Machado 10, Benalmádena Costa
☎ 952 44 12 95

Avenida San Lorenzo 1, Estepona
☎ 952 80 09 13

Avenida Jesús Santos Rein 6, Fuengirola
☎ 952 46 74 57
www.fuengirola.org

Pasaje de Chinitas 4, Málaga
☎ 952 21 34 45

Glorieta de la Fontanilla, Marbella
☎ 952 77 14 42
www.marbella.es

Calle Puerta del Mar 4, Nerja
☎ 952 52 15 31

Avenida Marqués del Duero 69, San Pedro de Alcántara
☎ 952 78 52 52

Avenida de Andalucía 52, Torre del Mar
☎ 952 54 11 04

Ayuntamiento, Plaza Blas Infante 1, Torremolinos
☎ 952 37 95 12

NATIONAL HOLIDAYS

JAN	FEB	MAR	APR	MAY	JUN	JUL	AUG	SEP	OCT	NOV	DEC
2	1	1	1	1	1	1	1	0	1	1	3

1 Jan	New Year's Day
6 Jan	Epiphany
28 Feb	Andalucian Day (regional)
Mar/Apr	Maundy Thursday, Good Friday, Easter Monday
1 May	Labour Day
24 Jun	San Juan (regional)
25 Jul	Santiago (regional)
15 Aug	Assumption of the Virgin
12 Oct	National Day
1 Nov	All Saints' Day
6 Dec	Constitution Day
8 Dec	Feast of the Immaculate Conception
25 Dec	Christmas Day

OPENING HOURS

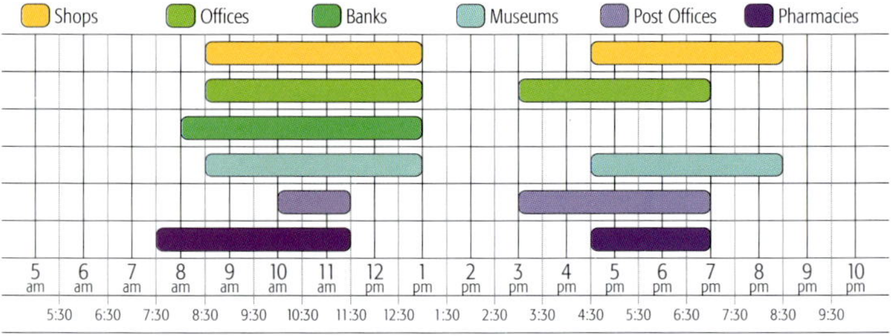

In addition to the times shown above, department stores, large supermarkets and shops in tourist resorts open from 10am through to 8, 9 or even 10pm. Most shops close Sunday and some in August. Most banks open 9–2 (Mon–Fri). Some banks open Sat 9–2 (Oct–May). The opening times of museums can vary: some open longer in summer, while hours may be reduced in winter. Many museums close Sunday afternoon, some also on Saturday afternoon, as well as Monday or another day in the week. Some museums offer free entry to EU citizens (take your passport). **All opening times are subject to change.**

PERSONAL SAFETY

Snatching of handbags and cameras, pick-pocketing, theft of unattended baggage and car break-ins are the principal crimes against visitors. Any crime or loss should be reported to the national police force (Policía Nacional) who wear brown uniforms. Some precautions:

- Do not leave valuables on the beach or poolside
- Place valuables in a hotel safety-deposit box
- Wear handbags and cameras across your chest
- Avoid lonely, seedy and dark areas at night

Police assistance: ☎ 091 from any call box

PUBLIC TRANSPORT

Internal Flights The national airline, Iberia, plus the smaller Aviaco, operate an extensive network of internal flights. The main office of Iberia is at Calle Molina Larios 13, Málaga (☎ 952 13 61 47). For reservations on domestic flights (☎ 901 33 31 11). Not cheap but worth considering if in a hurry.

Trains Services are provided by the state-run company – RENFE. Fares are among the cheapest in Europe. A useful service is the coastal route from Málaga to Fuengirola, via Torremolinas and Benalmádena, with a stop at the airport. Trains run every 30 minutes between 6am and 11pm (RENFE Málaga ☎ 952 12 82 63 or 952 36 02 02).

Buses There is a comprehensive and reliable bus network operated by different companies along the coast and to inland towns and villages. Fares are very reasonable. Go to the local bus station for details of routes. The bus station in Málaga (☎ 952 35 00 61) is just behind the RENFE train station.

Ferries A service runs from Málaga to Melilla (Morocco), run by Trasmediterránea Málaga (☎ 902 45 46 45), taking 10 hours. A shorter route to Morocco is from Algeciras to Ceuta (11/2 hours) and Tangier – via Gibraltar – (2.5 hours) run by ISNASA (☎ 956 65 37 06), Trasmediterránea (☎ 956 66 52 00), and Transtour (☎ 956 65 37 06).

Urban Transport Traffic in the main towns and resorts of the Costa del Sol is normally heavy, especially in summer, but public transport in the form of buses is generally good. From the RENFE station there is a bus which runs ervery 10 minutes or so to the city centre.

DRIVING

Speed limits on *autopistas* (toll motorways) and *autovías* (free motorways): **120kph**; dual carriageways and roads with overtaking lanes: **100kph**. Take care on the N340 coastal highway. Cars travel at tremendous speed and this road is labelled as a dangerous one.

Speed limits on country roads: **90kph**

Speed limits on urban roads: **50kph**; in residential areas: **20kph**

Seatbelts must be worn in front seats at all times and in rear seats where fitted.

Random breath-testing. Never drive under the influence of alcohol.

Fuel (*gasolina*) is available in four grades: *Normal* (92 octane); *Super* (98 octane); *Sin plomo* (unleaded, 95 and 98 octane); and *gasoleo* or *gasoil* (diesel). Petrol prices are fixed by the Government and are similar to those in the UK. Most take credit cards.

If you break down with your own car and are a member of an AIT-affiliated motoring club, call the Real Automóvil Club de España, or RACE (☎ 915 94 74 00; fax 915 94 72 49) for assistance. If the car is hired you should follow the instructions in the documentation; most international rental firms provide a rescue service.

CAR RENTAL

The leading international car rental companies operate on the Costa del Sol and you can hire a car in advance (essential at peak periods) either direct or through a travel agent. Airlines may offer 'fly-drive' deals. Hiring from a local firm, though, is usually cheaper.

TELEPHONES

All telephone numbers throughout Spain now consist of nine digits (incorporating the former area code, preceded by 9), and no matter where you call from you must always dial all nine digits. Most public telephones take coins and phonecards (*tarjetas telefónicas*) which are sold at *tabacos* or post offices for 6 or 12 euros. Some also accept credit cards.

International Dialling Codes

From Spain to:

UK: 00 44
USA: 00 1
Germany: 00 49
Netherlands: 00 31

POST

Post Offices

Post offices (*correos*) are generally open as below; in main centres they may open extended hours. Málaga's main post office is at Avenida de Andalucía 1. Stamps (*sellos*) can also be bought at tobacconists (*estancos*).

Open: Mon–Sat 9–2 (1pm Sat) ☎ 902 29 72 97 (Málaga)

TIPS/GRATUITIES

Yes ✓ No ✗

Restaurants (if service not included)	✓	5–10%
Cafés/bars	✓	change
Taxis	✓	2–3%
Tour guides	✓	change
Porters	✓	change
Chambermaids	✓	change
Hairdressers	✓	change
Cloakroom attendants	✓	change
Theatre/cinema usherettes	✓	change
Toilets	✓	change

HEALTH

Insurance Nationals of EU countries are entitled to some free medical treatment in Spain with the relevant documentation (Form E111 for Britons; a European Health Insurance Card will be issued to everyone in the UK applying for a new Form E111) although private medical insurance is still advised and is essential for all other visitors.

Dental Services Dental treatment normally has to be paid for in full as dentists operate privately. A list of *dentistas* can be found in the yellow pages of the telephone directory. Dental treatment should be covered by private medical insurance.

Sun Advice The sunniest (and hottest) months are July and August when daytime temperatures are often into the 30°s C. Try to avoid the midday sun and use a high-factor sun cream.

Drugs Prescriptions and non-prescription drugs and medicines are available from pharmacies (*farmácias*), distinguished by a large green cross. They are able to dispense many drugs which would be available only on prescription in other countries.

Safe Water Tap water is chlorinated and generally safe to drink; however, unfamiliar water may cause mild abdominal upsets. Mineral water (*agua mineral*) is cheap and widely available. It is sold *sin gas* (still) and *con gas* (carbonated).

ELECTRICITY

The power supply is: 220/230 volts (in some bathrooms and older buildings: 110/120 volts). Type of socket: round two-hole sockets taking round plugs of two round pins. British visitors will need an adaptor and US visitors a voltage transformer.

TAXIS

Only use taxis which display a licence issued by the local authority. Taxis show a green light when available for hire. They can be flagged down in the street. In cities and large towns taxis are metered; where they are not, determine the price of the journey in advance.

CONCESSIONS

Students/Youths Holders of an International Student Identity Card (ISIC) may be able to obtain some concessions on travel, entrance fees etc, but the Costa del Sol is not really geared up for students (special facilities and programmes are limited). The main advantage for students and young people is that low-cost package deals are available.

Senior Citizens The Costa del Sol is an excellent destination for older travellers – travel agents offer tailored package holidays. In the winter months there are special low-cost, long-stay holidays for senior citizens; the best deals are available through tour operators who specialise in holidays for senior citizens.

Index

INDEX

ACKNOWLEDGEMENTS

The Automobile Association would like to thank the following photo libraries for their assistance in the preparation of this book.

Corbis UK 214; **Bananastock** 167; **Photodisc** 67, 162, 174/5, 178, 219, 239

The remaining photographs are held in the Automobile Association's own Photo Library (AA World Travel Library) and were taken by the following photographers:

Michelle Chaplow 3br, 13, 22, 25, 26/7, 29, 39, 42, 47, 59, 74, 85, 94, 98/9, 103, 114, 116, 123, 134, 154, 194, 195, 232, 247; **Jerry Edmanson** 3bl, 19, 21, 36, 143, 150, 157; **Max Jourdan** 198/9, 211; **Simon McBride** 182; **Andrew Molyneux** 2tl, 144, 146, 147, 149, 190, 191, 227; **Jens Poulsen** 58, 62, 64, 82, 110; **Douglas Robertson** 14/5, 18, 28, 93, 118, 131, 170, 186/7, 231, 254/5; **James Tims** front cover, 1, 2bl, 2/3, 11, 34, 44, 51, 54, 81, 90, 102, 104, 107, 126, 129, 136, 138, 141, 155, 158/9, 160, 187, 202/3, 243, 246; **Clive Sawyer** 71, 183; **Wyn Voysey** 31, 87; **Peter Wilson** 17, 32, 101, 132.

Typesetting: **Information Engineers** Page layout: **Pentacor book design**
Editors: **Marilynne Lanng, Pam Stagg** Design support: **Katherine Mead**